MW01200411

Flowers of the Passion
St. Paul of the Cross

Flowers of the Passion
St. Paul of the Cross

Thoughts of Saint Paul of the Cross,

Founder of the Passionists.

Gathered from the Letters of the Saint
By REV. LOUIS TH. DE
JÉSUS-AGONISANT, of the same order.

Translated from the French
By Ella A. Mulligan.

New York, Cincinnati, Chicago:
Benzinger Brothers, printers to the
Holy Apostolic See

Republished by Jacob Stein

Filii Passionis
2018

First Printing: 2018

Filii Passionis
Rome, Italy
www.PassioXP.com

PREFACE TO THIS EDITION

A wise priest once instructed that I should spend 15 minutes a day at the Foot of the Cross. And that, in this short span of time, I should present to Christ everything! Everything of myself, everything of what Christ did for me, everything! Every joy, every hope, every care, every anxiety, every gratitude, every fear. Nothing should be held back before Christ and what more fitting place to tell Him than at the Foot of the Cross where He expresses His Thirst for me. This is the most profound relationship we can ever have.

Years later I would discover that Saint Paul of the Cross taught the same counsel this priest teaches. In addition to this counsel, this work is full of the wisdom of sanctity.

This devotional is presented by a group of Roman Catholic laymen aspiring to live a traditional monastic life according to the Rule of Saint Paul of the Cross. At the moment, the men do not live in community. It is their prayer that this will come to fruition soon for the sake of the glorification of God, their sanctification, the sanctification of others and the assistance of Holy Mother Church.

The prayers and sacrifices of these men are united to this Holy Rule of their father, Saint Paul of the Cross. According to their circumstances, they strive to apply the maxims of this Rule to daily life. In your charity, please pray for this endeavor of reform.

The devout inspiration of this group is the patrimony of Saint Paul of the Cross. This group of men will gather inspired as Saint Mary Magdalene was prior to the Passion of Our Blessed Lord.

It was she who gave example of how we should make reparation to Christ, Who in His Passion was spat upon, beaten, scourged, mocked. She understood, having turned from a life of sin by the gentle voice of Our Lord. She, with great sorrow for her sins, anointed our Lord's Head with precious ointment and bathed His Feet with her tears, knowing that His Love would move Him to lay down His life for her, for you. So men must gather to do the same, to make reparation to Our Blessed Lord for the sins of mankind, for their own sins, and come to know ever more deeply the Love of Christ in His Passion, in His Crucifixion, so that they may be led, and lead souls, to the glory of the Resurrection!

Saint Gemma is also a particular patroness of this endeavor. It is she who is called, in death, foundress of the Passionist monastery at Lucca, though the very order refused her entry, in life. She is a perennial model, but is a model especially for our times. Her love for the Passion and her love for the Blessed Sacrament were one and the same. Jesus in the Eucharist and Jesus on the Cross would be throughout Gemma's life the inseparable objects of her love. Sons of the Passion must gather also as sons of the Most Blessed Sacrament. They will love Christ in the Blessed Sacrament, the Gift given the night before He was betrayed. They will make reparation for this betrayal and for the lack of love and the many sacrileges and profanations against our Adorable Lord in the Blessed Sacrament. They will love Christ in the Eucharist, they will love Christ on the Cross!

May this devotional bear fruit in your spiritual life, in growing ever more profoundly in love with Love Crucified, through a greater encounter with the constant thought of you by Christ in His Life and in His Passion! In all things, He thought of you!

Our Lady of Sorrows, pray for us!
Saint Paul of the Cross, pray for us!
Saint John, brother of Paul, pray for us!
Saint Gabriel of Our Lady of Sorrows, pray for us!
Saint Mary Magdalene, pray for us!
Saint Gemma, pray for us!

In vulneribus Christi,

Jacob Stein
Feast of Saint George
23 April 2018

Table of Contents.

————

Flowers of the Passion

INTRODUCTION

These little "Flowers of the Passion" are a collection of devout thoughts and sentiments gathered mostly from occasional letters of that great lover of Jesus crucified, St. Paul of the Cross. They are a treasure to humble and simple souls, and show what sweetness, comfort, graces, and virtues can be drawn from devout meditation on the Passion and death of Jesus Christ. It is only from constant and loving reflection on the love shown towards us, and the bright examples of every virtue given us by our suffering Lord, that such beautiful and affecting sentiments could so spontaneously spring.

To enjoy, therefore, all the benefits to be derived from these exquisite little blossoms of love, we should imitate St. Paul of the Cross, and meditate in our own humble way on the mysteries of the sacred Passion of Our Lord.

Wherefore, to insure greater utility to the devout reader of these flowerets, we subjoin in an appendix a short instruction on the most easy and profitable method of meditating on the sufferings of Jesus Christ, Who became an outcast and a reproach among His people in order to atone for our sins, to reveal His love for us, and to give us a bright example of every virtue." Christ suffered for us, leaving you an example that you should follow His steps." (i Peter ii. 21).

PREFACE

Desiring to satisfy the piety of the faithful, we have gathered into one volume the fragments of the letters of St. Paul of the Cross which appear in the various histories of his life.

Even though these letters be incomplete, they suffice to reveal in St. Paul of the Cross a great master of the spiritual life, a sure guide in the way of perfection, a heart burning with divine love—in a word, a radiantly beautiful soul.

We know with what eagerness the literary world seeks to possess itself of the correspondence of celebrated men, that through their letters may be seen the interesting drama of their interior lives. Now if the children of the world do this to gratify mere human curiosity, surely the children of God may do likewise when there is question of unveiling the secrets of the divine action in the theatre of the Christian soul.

And what a charm there is in reading the interior lives of the friends of God!

Who that is familiar with them does not admire the spiritual letters of St. Francis de Sales, so full of wisdom, sweetness, and unction, as well as those of Bossuet, Fénelon, and many other teachers in the important and difficult art of the government of souls? St. Paul of the Cross deserves to rank with these grand spiritual directors; therefore we present this little treatise to the public.

To the letters we have added some reflections or maxims of the saint which ever and anon, like flashes of heavenly wisdom, escaped from his fervent soul; they are well calculated to enlighten and console others less favored than he.

St. Paul of the Cross was preeminently the preacher of the sufferings and Passion of Our Lord, and in entitling this volume "Flowers of the Passion" we believe we have given the true name to the beautiful sentiments that it embodies. It was on Calvary, on the holy mount, that the saint culled them. But let us remember that, in order to appreciate the beauty of these Flowers and inhale their sweet and salutary perfume, we must accept, at the risk of wounding our hands, the thorns which surround them and serve as their surety and safeguard. Such is the constant law of the spiritual life: the cross is sweet only to those who love it; and the profound joys of sacrifice

are reserved for souls who quail
not before its austerities.

FLOWERS OF THE PASSION

The Passion and the Way of Perfection

The Passion of Christ is the door which opens into the delicious pastures of the soul. Our divine Saviour has said: "I am the door. By Me if any man enter in, he shall be saved." (John x. 9).

*

Imagine yourself seriously indisposed, and that I, who love you tenderly, call to see you. After saying a few words of sympathy and consolation, I should certainly look at you with compassion and, through love of you, make your sufferings my own. Thus when we meditate on the Passion of Christ, seeing Him in such affliction, we ought to compassionate Him, and then to remain looking upon Him in so great torments, and, through compassionate love, make His sufferings our own.

Suppose that you had fallen into the river, and that a charitable person threw himself into the water to save you. What would you say to such kindness? Moreover, suppose that, hardly drawn from the water, you had been attacked by assassins, and that your rescuer again came to your assistance, and saved your life at the risk of his own. What would you do in return for such friendship? It is certain that you would do all in your power to heal the bruises he received on your account. So ought we to act towards Christ: we must contemplate Him engulfed in an ocean of sorrows to save us from the eternal abyss; consider Him all covered with wounds and bruises to purchase for us eternal life. Then let us make His pains our own, sympathize with His sorrows, and consecrate to Him all our affections.

*

Keep a continual remembrance of the sufferings of your heavenly Spouse. Endeavor to fathom the love with which He endured them. The shortest way is to lose yourself completely in that abyss of sufferings. Truly does the prophet call the Passion of Jesus a sea of love and of sorrow. Ah! therein lies the great secret which is revealed only to humble souls. In this vast sea the soul fishes for the pearls of virtues, and makes her own the sufferings of her Beloved. I have a lively confidence that your Spouse will teach you this divine method of fishing; He will teach it to you if you keep yourself in interior solitude, your

mind free from all distraction,
detached from all earthly affection,
from every created thing, in pure
faith and holy love.

*

Hold yourself interiorly on
the bosom of God, in the passive
way; this is the surest means of
losing yourself in God, passing,
however, continually through the
Gate divine, which is Jesus Christ
crucified, making His sufferings
yours. *Love teaches all*, for the
Passion with its bitter sorrows is the
work of infinite love.

*

How can you, by love, make
your own the sufferings of our
sweet Jesus? God will teach you
how when it pleases Him, for He
alone can do so. The soul inflamed
with the love of God, without
distraction, in pure and simple

faith, suddenly finds herself, when God pleases, penetrated with the sufferings of Jesus; in a glance of faith she sees them all, without understanding; for the Passion of Our Saviour is a labor of love, and the soul thus lost in God, Who is all charity, all love, makes of herself a fount of love and sorrow.

*

Our sweet Jesus has pierced your heart so deeply with the thorns of His sorrows that you will say henceforth: To suffer and not to die! or else: To suffer or to die! or better still: Neither to suffer nor to die, but entire submission to the good pleasure of God. Love has an unitive quality, and makes the sufferings of the beloved its own. If you feel yourself penetrated interiorly and exteriorly with the sufferings of your divine Spouse, rejoice; but I may say that this joy

is experienced only in the furnace
of divine love, for the fire which
burns into the marrow of the bones
transforms the loving soul into the
object of her love; and there, love
and   sorrow   are   so   sublimely
blended that the one can no longer
be distinguished from the other,
and the loving soul rejoices in her
sorrow, and finds her happiness in
her dolorous love. Persist in the
study of your nothingness, and be
faithful in the practice of virtue,
above all in the imitation of our
sweet Saviour in His patience, for
this is the cardinal point of pure
love.   Never   neglect   to   offer
yourself as a holocaust to the
infinite goodness of God. This
sacrifice ought to be made in the
fire of divine charity; light it with a
bouquet of myrrh, that is, with the
sufferings of your Saviour. All this
should be done behind closed

doors, that is, apart by yourself, in pure and simple faith.

*

In times of aridity arouse your spirit gently, by acts of love; then rest in the will of God. It is thus that the soul gives the strongest proof of her fidelity to God. Make a bouquet of the sufferings of Jesus, and place it on the bosom of your soul, as I have told you. You can from time to time call them to mind, and say sweetly to your Saviour: O good Jesus, how swollen, bruised, and defiled with spittle do I behold Thy countenance! O my Love! why do I see Thee all covered with wounds? O Infinite Sweetness! why are Thy bones laid bare? Ah, what sufferings! what sorrows! O my God! for what art Thou all wounded! Ah, dear sufferings, dear wounds! I wish to keep you always in my heart.

*

Wear, if you wish, a necklace of pearls when you go out; but when you put it on remember that Jesus wore the rope and the heavy chain about His neck. Wear that pearl necklace only in order to please God, and humble yourself by saying Jesus was bound with ropes and heavy chains during His Passion, and I wear pearls.

*

The days of the Passion are days when the very stones melt into tears. What! the High Priest is dead, and we cannot weep over Him? We must have lost faith, O my God!

*

The thought of Friday is suggestive of reflections so sad as to make one that truly loves, sorrowful unto death; for was it not on that day that my Incarnate God suffered for me, even to immolating Himself for me, on the infamous gibbet of the cross?

*

Let us always wear mourning in our hearts, in memory of the Passion and death of Jesus. We should never fail to preserve a continual and sorrowful remembrance of it. Let each of us endeavor to lead others to meditate on the sufferings of our most sweet Jesus.

*

[St. Paul of the Cross writing to a spiritual daughter in the days leading up to the Holy Triduum]:

My very dear child in Jesus crucified, I invite you to Calvary, to assist at the obsequies of Our Saviour. Ah! would that we could, for once, remain there, wounded by divine charity wounded so deeply as to die of love and sorrow over the Passion and death of our only Good! I will celebrate the divine mysteries during these holy days, and each time I do so I will place the heart of this spiritual child whom God has given me in the most pure and agonizing Hearts of Jesus and Mary. Do likewise for the poor spiritual father whom divine Providence has given to you. Adieu, my child; and may Jesus bless you, and inflame you with divine love.

The Passion and the Crucifix

When you are alone in your room, take your crucifix, kiss its five wounds reverently, tell it to preach you a little sermon, and then listen to the words of eternal life that it speaks to your heart; listen to the pleading of the thorns, the nails, the precious Blood. Oh, what an eloquent sermon!

*

The festival of the cross may be celebrated at every moment in the interior sanctuary of the true lovers of the crucifix. And how may it be celebrated? I will explain to you as best I can. We celebrate this feast spiritually by suffering in silence, without leaning on any creature; and as feasts are kept with joy, the festival of the cross ought to be kept by the lovers of the crucifix by suffering in silence, with a countenance happy and serene, in order that the pain may be hidden from the eyes of creatures and be known only to God. In this feast we feed at a delicious banquet, nourishing ourselves in the divine Will, in imitation of our crucified Love. Oh, what sweet food! It is composed of various elements: mental and physical sufferings, contradictions, calumnies, contempt, etc. Oh, how deliciously these things taste to the spiritual palate, if they be taken in pure faith and holy love, in silence and with confidence!

An angel offered me, one day, a cross made of gold, to teach me the value of tribulations.

PSALM OF LOVE.

By the cross God perfects the loving soul that offers Him a fervent and generous heart.

Oh, what can I say of the precious and divine treasure that our great God has hidden in suffering?

But this is a great secret, known only to him who loves; and I, who have had no experience of it, must be content to admire it from afar.

Happy the heart that keeps itself on the cross, in the arms of the Well-Beloved, and that burns only with divine love!

Happier the one that suffers without joy, and is thus transformed into Christ!

Happy he who suffers without being attached to his suffering, desiring only to die to himself, in order to love yet more Him Who inflicts the wound of love!

I give you this lesson from the foot of the cross, but it is in prayer that you will understand it.

*

Christ prayed for three hours on the cross; this was truly a crucified prayer, without either interior or exterior consolation. O God! what a grand lesson! Beg God to impress it on your heart. Oh, how much food for meditation! While Jesus agonized on the cross He spoke His first three words, which were three arrows of love; and then He kept silence until the ninth hour, praying during the entire interval. I leave you to consider how devoid of consolation was this prayer.

*

Repose on the naked cross, and make no other complaint than this infantine cry: My Father, my Father, Thy will be done! and then be silent. Continue to repose on the cross until the happy moment of your mystical death. This precious death is more desirable than life. Then, as St. Paul said, your life will be hidden with Christ in God (Col. iii. 3), and you will find yourself in this profound solitude that you love, and entirely despoiled of every created thing. Now is the moment to suffer in silence and in peace; resign yourself to the agony you suffer, and it will conduct you to mystical death.

*

The life of the servants of God is a continual death. For you are dead and your life is hid with Christ in God. I wish you to die this mystical death. We have just celebrated the birth of Our Lord, and I am confident that you are born mystically in Christ daily, more and more; and I desire you to die in Him in a mystical manner, from day to day, more perfectly, and to dissipate, in the abyss of the

Divinity, all those little distractions that annoy you.

He who is mystically dead seeks only God, Who is so good and so great. He casts away all other thoughts, however good, in order to think only of God. He patiently awaits the ordinances of God; he ignores all else, that there may be no obstacle to the divine operation which is effected in the secret of the soul—there where no creature, neither angelic nor human, may approach; for God alone dwells in this secret place, which is the essence, the spirit, the sanctuary of the soul, where the heavenly hosts themselves are attentive to this divine operation, to this divine birth, which takes place every moment for him who is so happy as to be mystically dead on the cross.

There is where I study my sermon—at the foot of the crucifix.

*

May the holy cross of Christ remain ever planted in our heart! May our mind be grafted on this tree of life, and may it produce worthy fruits of penance, through the merits of the death of the true Author of life!

*

Your cross is indeed great! Thanks to our only Good, Who holds you on the cross! O beloved cross! O holy cross, tree of life, whence springs eternal life, I salute thee, I embrace thee, I press thee to my heart! Ah! these are the sentiments which ought to animate us in our trials. Courage, then! courage! Under so heavy a weight human nature will waver, it is true; but the soul will taste a sweet peace in the bosom of God.

Do not consider the magnitude of your trials; contemplate rather Jesus, your crucified Love,

the King of sorrows and of
anguish. If you do this, all your
sufferings will be flavored with
sweetness. Lift up your heart. Fix
your heart on God. For the time
being, you cannot, I admit, apply
yourself to prayer or to other
exercises of piety; but, with my
confidence founded on Christ, I
will give you a rule which will
enable you to pray without
ceasing: He prays always who
lives well. Animate yourself with
faith, I beg of you; keep yourself in
the presence of God in all your
actions.

On awaking, keep your heart
under control, by the remembrance of God, your Love, your
only Good. When God inspires
you with a sentiment of love, stop
and taste it, as the bee sips the
honey...Ah! when I reflect that my
soul is the temple of God, that God
dwells in me, how my heart

rejoices! All affliction appears to me sweet and light...What a fruitful source of meditation!

Live in the joy and the peace of the divine Majesty. Live lost in divine love. Live for divine love and of divine love.

O cherished cross! Through thee my most bitter trials are replete with graces!

*

O souls! seek a refuge, like pure doves, in the shadow of the crucifix. There mourn the Passion of your divine Spouse, and drawing from your hearts flames of love and rivers of tears, make of them a precious balm with which to anoint the wounds of your Saviour.

The Passion and the Holy Eucharist

O Lord, how sweet is Thy Spirit! "I know whom I have believed, and I am certain." (2 Tim. i. 12). I am certain that Thou art in the tabernacle. What happiness to remain during the most silent hours at the foot of the altar! Oh, who will give me the wings of a dove, that I may take my flight of love towards Thy divine Heart?

*

It is no time to speak to creatures when we are before the Eucharistic throne where dwells the Lord of lords, the Master of the world.

*

Each time that you celebrate Mass or approach the holy Table, imagine that you are receiving the Viaticum.

*

Do not neglect to make due preparation for the Holy Sacrifice; always make your thanksgiving; watch day and night over the interior tabernacle, that is, the heart of the worthy priest. He who acts thus will not fail to enkindle within himself the fire of divine love. Guard cautiously this living tabernacle, and keep always burning the lamps of faith and charity. May it be ever adorned with virtues! Imitate the perfect dispositions of your Saviour. Since the Mass is the renewal of the Sacrifice of the Cross, enter into the sentiments of compunction and of love which animated the Blessed Virgin, St. John, Joseph of Arimathea, and Nicodemus. The heart of the priest ought to be the sepulchre of Christ. As the tomb in which He was laid after death was new, so ought your heart be pure, animated with a lively faith, a firm confidence, an ardent charity, a fervent desire for the glory of God and the salvation of souls. The Mass is the most favorable occasion to treat with the eternal Father, because then we offer Him His only Son as a victim for our salvation. Before celebrating, reflect on the sufferings of your Redeemer, commune peaceably with Him, even in the midst of dryness; carry to the altar the needs of the entire world.

*

Do not pass a single day without visiting the God of the tabernacle; in His presence grieve for the irreverences that He receives from bad Christians, who repay His love with sacrileges and basest ingratitude. In reparation for so many outrages, the loving soul ought to offer herself as a victim, consume herself in the fire of divine love, offer her praises to

Jesus on the altar, visit Him for those unhappy souls who fail to do so, visit Him especially at hours when nobody else pays Him homage.

*

The feast of the Blessed Sacrament is the feast of love. Oh, what great love! what immense charity! The moth is drawn to the light, and burns itself in it. May your soul likewise draw near to the divine light! May it be reduced to ashes in that sacred flame, particularly during this great and sweet octave of Corpus Christi.

Ah! eat, drink, run, sing, rejoice in honor of your divine Spouse.

*

How wonderful are the treasures which are enclosed in the divine Eucharist!

I exhort you, though you live in the world, to communicate often, but with piety.

Holy Communion is the most efficacious means of uniting one's self to God.

Always prepare yourself well for this sacred banquet. Have a very pure heart, and watch over your tongue, for it is on the tongue that the Sacred Host is laid. Carry Our Lord home with you after your thanksgiving, and let your heart be a living tabernacle for Jesus. Visit Him often in this interior tabernacle, offering Him your homage and the sentiments of gratitude with which divine love will inspire you.

Preserve carefully the sentiments of love with which you are filled after Communion.

You could not love Jesus if you did not possess the living source of holy and pure love, namely, the Holy Spirit. Our divine Redeemer said, "He that believeth in Me, out of his belly shall flow streams of living water." (John vii. 38). This He said of the spirit which they should receive who believed in Him. Therefore, when God enkindles in you the flames of divine love, holy, pure, and without stain, let yourself disappear in the infinite Good, and, like an infant, sleep the sleep of faith and love in the bosom of your heavenly Spouse.

*

Love speaks little.

*

The hermits of old, those great servants of God, communicated rarely; but because they prepared themselves carefully they received such special graces that, in a short time, they arrived at perfection.

*

Every day make a visit to the Blessed Sacrament, and when the duties of your state of life prevent you, visit Him in spirit.

*

The Holy Eucharist very often invigorates and strengthens even the body. O infinite mercy of our sovereign Good! this marvelous effect proceeds from the great vigor which the bread of angels communicates to the soul, and which reacts on the body.

*

O Jesus, hidden under the Eucharistic veils, Thou hast said: "If any one thirst, let him come to Me, and I will refresh him." Do Thou quench my thirst...In truth, in truth, Jesus has refreshed me; at some future day He will entirely quench my thirst.

*

My God, the tabernacle is the abode of Thy love, prepared by

Thee for those whom Thou lovest. When shall I be enabled, during the hours of profound solitude, to commune with my Eucharistic Love at the foot of the holy altar? Who will give me the wings of a dove, that I may take my flight to the Sacred Heart of Jesus?

The Passion and Spiritual Infancy

"Put off the old man with his works, and put ye on the Lord Jesus Christ."

God delights in those who make themselves little and become as little children; He keeps them near His person, and nourishes them with the milk of divine love, in order to prepare them for the sweet wine of holy love, which inebriates those who drink it; but it is a blessed wine, which gives daily more wisdom.

*

Let us make ourselves as children with Jesus, hiding ourselves in our nothingness; let us be humble and simple as children by an exact obedience, by purity of heart, by love of holy poverty by a love of sufferings, and, above all, by childlike

simplicity in the faithful
observance of our rules and
constitutions, and let us not take
the liberty to interpret them
broadly nor in any other sense
than their own. Narrow is the way
that leadeth to life. Let us allow
ourselves to be guided and used
by our superiors, whom God has
placed over us for our government
and direction.

Thus we shall be true
imitators of the Child Jesus, Who
abandoned Himself in everything
to the care of His Mother the most
holy and immaculate Virgin Mary.

By these beautiful virtues
you will render yourselves worthy
to partake of the banquet of angels.

At this sacred banquet
contemplate the divine Child,
trembling with cold, which He
suffered that He might enkindle in
our hearts the flames of divine
love. Ah! ponder attentively this

grand mystery. Consider the inconveniences, the cold, the poverty, the absence of all comforts which Jesus, Mary, and Joseph endured; and I hope that through the goodness of God, you will form the generous resolution of becoming great saints by the faithful imitation of Jesus, Mary, and Joseph.

Model your hearts on that of the divine Infant, that He may vivify you, encourage you, inflame you, sanctify you, render you capable of doing great things for the glory of God; and may the holy Virgin keep you pure with the precious balm of her virtues! Amen.

*

O Jesus, my Love, may my heart be consumed in loving Thee; make me humble and holy; give me childlike simplicity; transform me into thy holy love. O Jesus, life of my life, joy of my soul, God of my heart, accept my heart as an altar, on which I will sacrifice to Thee the gold of ardent charity, the incense of continual, humble, and fervent prayer, and the myrrh of constant mortification! Amen.

The Passion and the Virgin Mary

The great heart of the child Mary is, after the Heart of Jesus, the holiest of all hearts; it has loved, and it loves God more than the whole court of heaven, more than all the angels and saints, past, present, and to come. Desire, then, to love God like the heart of this sublime child, and to this end place yourself in this beautiful heart, and love God through it, with the intention of practicing all the virtues of which it has given us the example.

*

How can we form an adequate idea of Mary's triumph on the occasion of her glorious Assumption?

*

The riches of this great Queen are immense; she is an

ocean of perfection, the depth of which can be fathomed only by Him Who has enriched it with so many graces.

The wonderful wound of love which she received at the instant of her Immaculate Conception went on ever enlarging, during life, until finally it penetrated her so profoundly that it detached her most holy soul from her body. Thus it was a death of love, sweeter than life itself, which ended the boundless sorrow that she suffered in the course of her earthly pilgrimage, not only during the Passion of Christ, but also in witnessing the offenses and ingratitude of men towards the divine Majesty. Let us, then, rejoice in God, over the signal triumph of Mary, our Queen and Mother; let us rejoice in seeing her raised above the choirs of angels and placed at the right hand of her divine Son. You may extol the glories of Mary in the Sacred Heart of Jesus, and even love her with this divine Heart; and, if Jesus permit you, take flight into the Immaculate Heart of Mary, rejoice with her, congratulate her that her sufferings are at an end, ask grace to live always immersed in that immense ocean of divine love whence springs that other ocean of the sufferings of Jesus and the dolors of Mary. Let us be pierced through by those sufferings and these dolors; and let the sword be well tempered, that the wound of love may be the deeper; for the deeper it is, the sooner will the captive soul escape from her prison. I am in an abyss of darkness, and I know not how to speak of these marvels. He who would be the most pleasing to Mary must humble himself the most, for Mary was the humblest of creatures, and for that reason she pleased God more than all others.

Meditate frequently on the sorrows of the Mother of God sorrows inseparable from those of her beloved Son. If you go to the crucifix, you will there find the Mother, and, on the other hand, wherever the Mother is, there, also, is the Son.

*

Unite the sufferings of Jesus with those of the holy Virgin, and, bowing yourself beneath their weight, make of yourself a holocaust of love and sorrow. Divine love will teach you how, if you keep yourself concentrated in your nothingness.

*

Today we commemorate the dolors of Mary; recommend me fervently to her, that her dolors and the Passion of my Jesus may be ever graven on my heart. I wish it with all the ardor of my soul. Would that I could impress them on the hearts of all men; then the whole world would be inflamed with divine love.

My heart breaks when I think of the sorrows of the most holy Virgin.

O tender Mother, unutterable was thy grief in finding thyself deprived of thy dear Son, and then in beholding Him dead in thy arms!

Ah! who can realize the sadness of Mary when she returned to Bethany after the burial of her Son?

Jesus expires on the cross! He is dead that we may have life. All creation mourns: the sun darkens, the earth trembles, the rocks burst, and the veil of the temple is rent in twain; my heart alone remains harder than a rock!

*

All I say to you now is, console the poor Mother of Jesus. It is a miracle that she does not die; she is absorbed in the sufferings of Jesus. Imitate her, and ask Magdalen and the beloved disciple St. John what are their sentiments.

*

I dwell in spirit at the foot of the cross.

*

The sorrow of May is like the Mediterranean Sea, for it is written, "Your sorrow is great as the sea." From that sea we pass to a second sea, which has no limits; it is the Passion of Our Lord, of which the Royal Prophet said, "I am entered on the high sea." There the soul enriches herself in fishing for the priceless pearls of virtue.

*

O immaculate Virgin, Queen of martyrs! I conjure thee, by the sorrows that thou didst endure during the awful Passion of thy amiable Jesus, give to all of us thy maternal blessing.

I place all my spiritual children under the mantle of thy protection.

The Passion and Prayer

I.

I would believe myself to have failed in duty, as St. Bonaventure said, were I to pass a single day without thinking of my Saviour's Passion.

*

Your most important business is the care of your soul. This is why, before leaving your room in the morning, you should spend at least a quarter of an hour meditating on the life, the Passion, and the death of Our Lord Jesus Christ.

*

Oh, what joy will it give to the blessed in heaven, and what pleasure to your guardian angel, to see you engaged in mental prayer! Never omit this holy exercise.

*

I would like the subject of your prayers to be the Passion of Jesus; let your heart lose itself in God in those loving communings. But understand me well; I wish you to leave your soul entirely free to follow the attractions of the Holy Spirit. I repeat to you, then, that we must pray, not according to our own fancy, but as God wills. Yes, when the soul is inclined to be alone with God, in pure and simple faith, reposing on the bosom of her Well-Beloved, in a silence begotten of love, silence in which the soul speaks to God much better than by words—in this case she must be left in peace, and not be disturbed by other exercises.

God then holds her in the arms of His love, and nourishes her with the delicious wine which generates virgins.

*

Sometimes, in prayer, God communicates to the soul, all at once, His treasures of lights and heavenly graces. Imagine that you have in your hand a golden dish, that you pour into it the extract of the rarest and most exquisite perfumes, and that you steep into it a fine cambric handkerchief; this handkerchief will yield a delicious and inexplicable odor, composed of all the perfumes. It is thus my soul feels when I receive those intimate and hidden communications.

*

Oh, how I wish that everybody would apply himself to meditation and prayer!

What a misfortune that there are so few souls who know the hidden treasure contained in prayer and union with God!

Alas! we enter easily on the road to perdition when we neglect prayer.

*

If God grants you the gift of prayer, be faithful to it; take care, however, that you do not become slothful in the practice of virtues and the imitation of Jesus.

Always begin your prayer with one of the mysteries of the Passion, and engage your soul in it by pious soliloquies, without making an effort to meditate. If God afterwards attract you to the silence of love and faith, do not disturb the peace of your soul by any explicit reflections. I advise you, above all things, to ground yourself in humility and in the hatred of yourself. Of this we can never do enough.

*

Be faithful to correspond with the wonderful graces which

you have received from Our Lord;
they are a preparation for greater
graces and more sublime lights,
which will cause you to love God
more, to acquire more solid virtue,
and to practice it in a more heroic
degree.

Truly, the more the soul is
enlightened by faith and prayer,
the more intimately is she united
to God, and by means of this union
with the Supreme Being she is
enriched with all goods, and she
accomplishes great things with
humility and a sense of her own
insufficiency. Thus she disposes
herself to be all absorbed in God in
contemplation, for the divine
Lover draws her to Himself by
means of this union.

It is for this reason that I
wish you to be diligent in the
study of your own nothingness,
that this nothingness may be

absorbed, so to speak, in the immensity of God, Who is all.

O happy loss! The soul finds herself again, indeed, after losing herself in God.

*

Ah! the God of truth loves the truth. Now, he who knows his nothingness, and acknowledges it, knows the truth.

Through contemplation, which acquaints us with this great truth that we are nothing and that God is all, our soul is plunged into the infinite love of the Supreme Good.

Follow the rules which I have marked out for your direction in prayer according to the lights that God has given me.

The state of prayer, in which God has placed you, requires few words.

Love speaks little. The language of divine love is a

burning heart; no words can express its ardors; they make of the loving soul a victim of love, a holocaust, consumed and reduced to ashes in the divine fire of charity.

*

My soul is entirely oblivious of self in that immense ocean of the infinite glories of God.

*

Let us be generous, let us serve the Lord nobly, let us practice great virtues; God will be our strength and will give us victory.

I recommend you not to lose sight of the Passion and death of Jesus, our life.

*

Remember that you ought no longer to meditate as you did in the beginning, but after the rules I have given you.

Love is an unitive virtue which appropriates the sufferings of the Beloved.

Meditate in pure faith; spend not your time in vain imaginings.

*

Make a nosegay of the sufferings of Jesus, and wear it on your bosom, or else keep yourself absorbed in God in pure faith let your soul be rapt in the thought of His sufferings and His love. Remain in this sacred silence, in this holy admiration, which increases the love of God.

*

I do not tell you to pray in my way, but in that of God. Leave your soul at liberty to receive the divine impressions according to God's pleasure.

We should pray according to the dictates of the Holy Spirit.

*

If God wishes to despoil us, let us allow Him to do so. Let us not neglect the practice of virtues, let us not neglect the holy presence of God, let us not neglect the remembrance of the Passion of our dear Jesus; but in meditation we must follow His inspirations, not our own impulses. There are some rules, but God is the Master.

Let us abandon ourselves to Him, trust in Him, despoil ourselves of everything, and God will clothe us after His own way.

*

Leave your soul free to take her flight to the Sovereign Good as God shall guide her.

The moth flies round the flame and falls into it; let your soul be drawn into the divine light and consumed in it.

The Passion and Prayer

II.

I see that you can no longer meditate as heretofore, nor picture to yourself the scenes of Our Savior's Passion; your mind suffers when you try to constrain it; *Deo gratias!* Act, then, in this way: keep yourself in the presence of God, with a pure and simple consideration of His immense goodness, in a loving silence; rest your spirit in the paternal bosom of your God, and when recollection ceases, recall it gently by a loving ejaculation.

*

O amiable Goodness! O infinite Charity! O my God and my All! O supreme Sweetness! Make these aspirations, or any others, as God will inspire you; but remember that if, in making one of these ejaculations of love, your soul regain her peace and recollection in God, it is unnecessary to make a second; continue, rather, this silence, this repose of the soul in God, which includes excellently all the acts that we can ever make.

When, on the contrary, you do not feel this interior peace, or this recollection, the soul can no longer meditate. Make no effort to do so; you ought, however, always to keep up a loving attention to God in the superior part of the soul. In this case, remain before God, detached from all consolation, like a statue in its niche.

*

"The true adorers shall adore the Father in spirit and in truth." (John iv. 23). Note these words well, because they contain all the elements of prayer; its perfection consists not in the joys and sensible delights which it may produce, but in the spirit—that is, in a true, pure, and simple nakedness and poverty of spirit, detached from all sensible consolation, so that the spirit reposes, purely and simply, in the infinite Spirit of God. Our Lord adds: "and in truth"—that is to say, we must have a full consciousness of our nothingness, so as not to rob God of one iota of His glory.

See that child: after having fondled and caressed its mother, it lulls itself on her breast, continuing to move its tiny lips sucking the milk; so the soul, after having spent her affections, so to speak, ought to rest on the bosom of her heavenly Father, and not awaken from this sleep of faith and love without the permission of God.

*

You ought to forget yourself in God; let your spirit fall, as a drop of water, into that immense ocean of charity, to repose there and receive the divine communications, without losing sight of your nothingness. We learn all things in this divine solitude; we learn more things in this interior school by being silent than by talking. St. Mary Magdalen out of love fell at the feet of Jesus; there she was silent, she listened, she loved, she lost herself in love.

*

Take with you everywhere this spirit of prayer and interior recollection. Go out of yourself, and lose yourself in God; go out of time, and lose yourself in eternity.

I am at the seashore; a drop of water is suspended from my finger. I ask this water: Poor drop, where would you wish to be? It replies: In the sea. And what do I in answer to this appeal? I shake my finger and let the poor little drop fall into the sea. Now, I ask you, is it not true that this drop of water is in the sea? Certainly it is there; but go and seek it, now that it is lost in the ocean, its center. If it had a tongue, what would it say? Deduce the consequence and apply the parable to yourself. Lose sight of the heavens, the earth, the sea and its rivers, and all created things, and permit this soul that God has given you to lose herself in this infinitely great and good God Who is her first cause.

*

See if this grace of prayer, with which the Most High favors you, produces in you a better knowledge of your utter insufficiency.

*

Be careful to keep yourself hidden from creatures, and visible to God only, by an earnest desire for His greater glory, by a profound contempt of yourself, by the practice of all virtues, especially humility, patience, gentleness, peace of heart, and by a perfect evenness of temper towards all persons with whom you come in contact.

Prayer is never more perfect than when it ascends from the very depth and essence of the soul; we pray, then, in the spirit of God. This is a sublime language, but when God wills, He makes even the stones speak. Let the sovereign God reign in your spirit; there ought to be a reciprocal repose: God in you, and you in God. O sweet, O divine operation!

God nourishes Himself, let me say for want of a better word God nourishes Himself with your spirit, and your spirit sustains herself with the Spirit of God:

Jesus is my nourishment, and I am His. There is no illusion possible in this operation, because it is a labor of faith and love.

*

Your prayer ought to be continual. The place wherein we ought to pray is the spirit of God.

In God we should chant the divine praises; we should do all things in God.

Pray twenty-four hours every day – that is, perform all your actions with heart and mind raised to God, holding yourself in interior solitude, and reposing in God in pure faith.

When your poor, restless heart turns by the grace of God towards the divine light, and conceives a wish to fly thither and be consumed therein, speak to God with profound reverence and gratitude of the wonders He did in becoming incarnate, suffering and dying for us.

One or two loving words may cause the soul to become enraptured, languishing, fainting of love and sorrow.

*

If you cannot spend much time at prayer, no matter: to act well is always to pray well.

Be attentive to your duties, and at the same time be attentive to God by frequently purifying your heart in the immense ocean of divine love.

*

Take care that your prayer becomes more and more interior, in pure faith humble yourself, and seek no consolations but the great God Who gives them.

*

A word suffices, sometimes, to dispose us to mental prayer. "Our Father, Who art in heaven"

— pronounce those words, and then let the heart act.

*

If we are men of prayer, God will make use of us, although poor and miserable, for the greatest triumphs of His glory; unless we are men of prayer, we can accomplish no good.

The Passion and the Presence of God

Were any one to ask me, no matter at what moment, "Of what are you thinking?" it seems to me I could reply, "God alone occupies my mind."

*

Though I find myself in so wretched a condition that I feel as if I no longer possess faith, hope, or charity, nor even that natural light which other men enjoy, so that I seem to be like an animal, even then, were I asked of what I was thinking, I could truthfully say that in the depth of my soul I have God alone present with me.

*

It seems to me impossible not to think of God, our soul being filled with God and we absorbed in God. In the *Pater Noster* do we not say, "Who art in heaven"? Ah well! our soul is a spiritual heaven; there the Divine Majesty has His throne. How, then, is it possible to forget God, or not to love Him?

*

I recommend to you particularly to keep yourself in the presence of God, not by a dry and sterile study, but affectionately and peaceably, in order to imbibe His spirit. This practice is a powerful means of establishing, between God and the soul, a holy union of charity.

*

"Walk before Me and be perfect." (Gen. xvii. I). Let everything recall to you the presence of God. If, for example, you go into the garden and see some flowers, ask one of them. What are you? It will not reply, I am a flower. No, but it will say to you, *Ego vox*—I am a preacher; I preach the power, the wisdom, the goodness, the beauty, the prudence of our great God.

Imagine that the flower makes you this reply, and let it penetrate your heart and teach you a lesson of divine love.

The Passion and Sin

How is it possible to offend a God scourged, a God crowned with thorns, a God crucified for us? And how is it possible that, seriously pondering these truths of faith, we can yet offend God?

I have converted by this means the most hardened sinners, and so sincere was their repentance that, when I afterwards heard their confessions, I could no longer find in them sufficient matter for absolution. So remarkable a change came about because they were faithful to the advice I had given them to meditate on the sufferings of Our Lord Jesus Christ.

*

Begin in the morning, before leaving your room, by meditating, for a quarter of an hour, on the

Passion of our Redeemer, and you will see that, all will go well with you, and that you will live far removed from sin.

*

The most efficacious means of converting the most obdurate sinners is the Passion of Our Lord, preached according to the method which Christ's vicar on earth has approved.

*

The greater number of Christians live unmindful of all that our most amiable Jesus has done and suffered. This is why they live on, sleeping in the horrible mire of iniquity. To arouse them from their detestable lethargy, it is necessary to send laborers burning with zeal, who with the trumpet of the divine Word, preaching the Passion of Christ, will awaken the poor sinners that are sitting in darkness and in the shadow of death.

*

Pray for our poor congregation, whose mission it is to mourn, without ceasing, the sorrows and the death of our beloved Redeemer. God wishes it to produce a great number of good laborers, who, as trumpeters of the Holy Ghost, will preach to the world and destroy sin.

The Passion and Heaven

From this valley of tears, turn your gaze continually to God, ever awaiting the moment when you will be united to Him in heaven. Often contemplate heaven, and fervently exclaim: What a beautiful abode there is above! It is destined for us! Sigh longingly after its possession. Sometimes say, while your eyes are moist with tears: Nothing in this world pleases me; I no longer care for anything but my God. Yes, I hope, yes, I wish to possess Him, and I hope this of the mercy of God, through the merits of my Saviour's Passion and the dolors of my good Mother Mary.

*

When you behold a beautiful landscape, say: Heaven is more beautiful than that! Above there are true delights and holy pleasures! Let us live, then, absorbed in the thought and the desire of that immense ocean of felicity which we are to enjoy in heaven.

*

How beautiful to look upon is the starry firmament! Yet it is only the portal of the blessed country where I hope to go one day.

Far from consoling me, the things of this world only inspire me with pain and disgust.

It seems to me that I am awaiting a thousand years the happiness of going to my God, my supreme good.

The soul, once in paradise, will be transformed into God, and God will be all in the soul, in such a manner that the soul will be, as it were, deified. Cast a drop of sweet water into the sea: it will be so absorbed that we can no longer distinguish it. So in heaven the beatified spirit, which is immersed in the immense ocean of the Divinity, is in a certain sense deified by being united, through love, to God.

*

Already the walls of the prison are crumbling to dust, and the prisoner is about to enjoy the liberty of the children of God.

Sigh after that happy country; leave your heart free to take its flight thither; above all, drink, with love, of your Saviour's chalice; inebriate yourself with it and how? By pure love and pure suffering; unite the two, or, rather, cast a drop of your sufferings into the ocean of divine love.

My son, in heaven the elect will not be united to me as a friend is united to a friend, but as the iron which is penetrated by the fire.

The Passion and Faith

Walk in faith.

Oh, how I love those souls who walk in pure faith, abandoning themselves entirely into the hands of God!

How I wish we would all walk in faith! Yes, this is the true way.

*

Obscure though faith be, it is the infallible guide of holy love. Oh, what delight my heart experiences in this certainty!

As St. John of the Cross said: O night, dark night, night more desirable than the break of day, night which unites the soul to God, and transforms her into her Well-Beloved!

*

Oh, what a noble practice to humble ourselves before God in

pure faith, and to lose our insignificant being in the infinite abyss of divine love!

*

Let us always seek God by faith in the interior of our soul.

Let a drop of rare perfume fall on a ball of cotton, and a delicious odor will be emitted from the entire ball; thus an aspiration of the heart to God embalms our soul with His divine spirit and causes her to emit a sweet odor in His presence.

Like infants let us rest on the bosom of God by faith, that we may enjoy His divine communications, and we will be fully satisfied.

*

Some there are whose devotion leads them to visit the holy places and the famous basilicas. I do not condemn this devotion; however, faith tells us that our heart is a great sanctuary, because it is the living temple of God and the abode of the Blessed Trinity. Let us enter this temple frequently, and there adore, in spirit and in truth, the august Trinity.

What a sublime devotion!

*

The kingdom of God is within you. Reanimate your faith often when you study, work, or eat; when you retire to rest, or rise in the morning. Make some loving aspirations to God, such as: "O Infinite Goodness!" or other prayer, and let your soul be penetrated by these pious senti-ments as by a precious balm. This great God is nearer to you, so to speak, than you are to yourself.

As for me, I cannot under-stand how it is possible not to be always thinking of God.

*

The just live by faith. You are the living temple of God. Visit this interior sanctuary often, and see that the lamps,—that is, faith, hope, and charity—are burning.

The Passion and Hope

Hope expands the heart, increases courage, and lovingly places us in the hands of God.

*

Fancy a mother who playfully holds in her arms a child over the edge of a high wall, or over the brink of a precipice. Who could believe that this mother would let her child fall? Neither can I persuade myself that God will let me fall into the depths of hell if I rely on Him; therefore I repose with perfect security on the bosom of Divine Goodness much more peacefully than does a child in the arms of its mother.

*

Place your hopes in the mercy of God and the merits of Our Redeemer; say often, looking at the crucifix: *There are centered all my hopes.*

*

I am full of miseries; however, I hope to save my soul: I hope it of the infinite power and goodness of God; I hope it through the Passion and death of Jesus; I hope it by the intercession of the Mother of Sorrows; yes, I hope to go to heaven.

*

If your eternal salvation depended on yourself alone, you would have serious cause for alarm, but since it is in the hands of your heavenly Father, what have you to fear? My hopes rest on the Passion of Jesus and on the dolors of Mary.

Why despair of your eternal salvation? Do you not know how good God is?

*

Let all our hopes center in the Infinite Goodness; let us give thanks to our Crucified Love when He deprives us of all human aid, and let us place still greater confidence in His fatherly goodness.

The Passion and Charity towards God

I ought to burn of love for God out of gratitude for the kindness that He has shown me.

*

If the Lord some day open my eyes to the dangers from which He delivered me, and the graces which He bestowed on me, you will find me dead of sorrow and love at the foot of the altar.

*

My only desire is to unite myself to my God.

*

It is impossible, to the human mind, to comprehend that infinite, eternal, immense Being; all that we can understand of Him in this life is nothing in comparison to the reality.

*

What! a God made man? a God crucified? a God dead? a God in the Sacrament of the Altar? Who? A God!

*

O charity! O marvels of love! And for whom? O ungrateful man! how is it possible that you do not love God?

*

Would that I could set the whole world on fire with the love of God!

Alas that I have not the strength to go and continue to preach my Jesus crucified, Who died on the cross for us sinners! Would that I might thus put an end to the commission of so many crimes!

*

I would fain say much, but in order to speak of love, it is necessary to love; love alone can suggest its own language.

Let the earth be silent before the great God. I repeat it: I would fain say many things, but I feel as one dumb.

Listen to your divine Spouse, and let yourself be taught by Him.

O my God! teach me how to express myself.

Would that I were all aflame with love! More than that: would that I could sing hymns of praise in the fire of love, and extol the marvelous mercies that uncreated love has bestowed on us! Is it not truly a duty to thank God for His gifts? Yes, doubtless, but I know not how. I wish to do so, and I know not how.

To faint away with the desire to love this great God more and more is little.

To consume ourselves for Him is little.

What shall we do? Ah! we will live for that divine Lover in a perpetual agony of love. But think you I have said enough? No; I would say more if I knew how.

Do you know what consoles me somewhat? To know that our great God is an infinite good, and that nobody is capable of loving and praising Him as much as He deserves.

I rejoice in the infinite love which He bears Himself; I rejoice in the essential happiness which He enjoys in Himself, without need of any creature. But, mad that I am, would it not be better for me to rush into those flames of love and there remain in silence, consumed and lost in that infinite All?

Ah! this is the work of love, and I am never sufficiently disposed to lose myself in love.

*

My heart now experiences such a thirst that a river would not suffice to satisfy it; an ocean is needed to quench this thirst, but it is an ocean of fire and love that I wish to consume.

*

When shall we be all on fire as are the seraphim? What shall we do to please our sweet Jesus? Ah! would that the fire of our charity were so great that it would inflame all who are near us, and all who are afar, all peoples, of every tongue and nation; in a word, all creatures, that all might know and love the Supreme Being!

*

In all your actions purify your intention, renew it several times a day, often repeat: *All for the greater glory of God!*

*

I would believe myself damned if I robbed God of one atom of His glory. I would believe myself more wicked than Lucifer if

I had anything else in view but God.

I recommend to you simplicity, purity of intention, and practical examen on this virtue; mark well that, in order to labor for the glory of God, our soul must be free and detached from all things, with God alone in view.

*

We must love God always, even when He sends us afflictions, looking up to God alone.

O my God, how good Thou art! I desire nothing else but Thee!

*

Divine love is a jealous love; one spark of irregular affection for any creature is sufficient to ruin all.

*

Let everything in creation draw you to God. Refresh your mind with some innocent recreation and needful rest, if it were only to saunter through the garden or the fields, listening to the sermon preached by the flowers, the trees, the meadows, the sun, the sky, and the whole universe. You will find that they exhort you to love and praise God that they excite you to extol the greatness of the Sovereign Architect Who has given them their being.

The Passion and the Love of Our Neighbor

You will find the name of Jesus engraven on the countenances of the poor.

Have courage, ye poor of Christ, because heaven is for the poor.

*

Wealth, unless it be devoted to good works, will become to its possessor only a source of endless torment in hell.

*

To provide for the sick, we should sell even our silver chalice.

*

If you succeed in bringing a single soul to heaven, what charity! what a gain! what glory to God!

*

If, during life, we have been kind to the suffering souls in purgatory, God will see that help be not denied us after death.

*

We must cover the failings of our neighbor with the mantle of charity, attributing them to ignorance or inadvertence.

*

You should regard the person that tries your patience as a treasure. Look upon her with an affectionate eye, as an instrument which God uses to clothe your soul with a garment of gold and pearls; that is, with the virtues, and especially with the patience, the silence, and the meekness of Christ. Oh, how much I cherish the trials which come to you through that person! Do not defend yourself, do not speak, or, if you say anything, let it be to excuse her and honor her. When you pass by her, bow your head respectfully as before an instrument in the paternal hand of God.

The better way is to be silent altogether, after the example of Christ.

*

Go in search of occasions to serve your accusers. You should seek these occasions more assiduously than people seek pearls and diamonds.

*

Do not be troubled because people despise and ignore me. God permits this trial to humble me, and I rejoice in it.

I know not what I have done to this prelate; I only know that I labored for a long time in his diocese, and that had I remained there I would have died. But the poor bishop merits sympathy, for persecutors and calumniators have not been lacking, especially since the question of establishing a retreat was broached. God be blessed! my trial does not trouble me. I intended to write to the bishop, but I am not equal to the task; it is much better to leave my justification to God. Love your enemies in Christ; show them the sweetest cordiality; at the same time make some interior act of love, as, for instance, "O dear souls of Jesus! I love you in the Heart of Jesus, which burns with love for you. O blessed souls! love Jesus for me."

The Passion and Poverty

Poverty is the glorious standard, the impregnable fortress of the religious life.

*

I recommend to you holy poverty; if you remain poor, you will be holy; on the contrary, if you seek to enrich yourselves, you will lose the religious spirit, and regular observance will disappear from your midst.

*

The children of the Passion of Jesus ought to be despoiled of all created wealth, and our Congregation should be distinguished by its poverty of spirit and perfect detachment from all things.

*

If the religious of the Congregation preserve the true spirit of poverty, the Congregation will maintain its vigor; I shall never cease to repeat it. If I were at the point of death, I should recommend three things; namely, to preserve the spirit of prayer, the spirit of solitude, and the spirit of poverty. Let the Congregation do this, and it will shine before God and men.

*

Poverty, of which the world has so great an abhorrence, imparts true joy and is a source of riches in the sight of God.

The Passion and Chastity

Possess purity in an eminent degree, and jealously preserve this fragrant flower. I earnestly desire to see you shine by the brilliancy of this virtue; be like to angels, and omit no precaution to retain this treasure, which is so easily lost by imprudence. We have this treasure in earthen vessels, says the Apostle. (2 Cor. x. 5).

*

I also recommend to you holy modesty at all times and in all places, because we are always in the presence of God, Who is everywhere. Let the admirable modesty of your Saviour be seen in your countenance, in your movements, and in your apparel.

I exhort you not only to watch over your eyes and to repress sensuality, but to conform your every movement to the rules of this virtue, which beautifies and ennobles every action.

*

Be faithful in all things to your heavenly Spouse, and live like innocent and stainless doves.

*

Avoid failing, not only against purity, but even against the least rules of an exact modesty.

*

The lily becomes whiter and sheds a sweeter fragrance among thorns than when growing in the open soil. In like manner, holy virginity becomes more beautiful and more pleasing to God amid the thorns of combats and temptations.

*

God permits that kind of temptation in order to impress you with a deeper sense of your own nothingness, and to convince you that, deprived of His grace, you would be capable of committing the most heinous crimes. Therefore act prudently, avoid all dangerous intercourse, watch over your eyes, your heart, and all your affections be very modest, be circumspect in all your actions, by night as well as by day; love holy modesty.

Do not act haughtily towards anybody, but, above all things, distrust yourself.

At night sprinkle your bed with holy water; retire to rest with the greatest modesty; have your crucifix at hand, and if you are assailed by any bad thought, kiss the five wounds, and strengthen yourself by saying: "Behold the cross of Jesus! Begone! infernal spirits. I command you to do so in the name of the Holy Trinity, in the name of Jesus, my Saviour, and of Mary, the Mother of God."

*

Distrust yourself, for we have seen the cedars of Libanus fall; distrust yourself always. It is necessary to fear, and to flee the occasions of sin. You must break off all intercourse with the person of whom you have spoken to me; I see there a secret attachment, and, under a specious pretext, either false zeal or the devil is laying a frightful snare for you, to cause you to fall down the precipice. In this kind of warfare we can conquer only by flight.

*

Prayer, good reading, the frequentation of the sacraments, with the proper dispositions, and particularly the flight of idleness— these are, believe me, the means of sanctifying yourself.

The Passion and Obedience

Ah! my beloved friends, practice, above all things, true and perfect charity; let it so unite your hearts that you may have only one heart and one will in God. Place yourselves entirely at the disposal of your superiors, that they may do with you what they will when they command nothing contrary to the law of God, or to the rules or constitutions, to which you must endeavor to remain always faithful.

Jesus, as you know, became obedient unto death, and the death of the cross. You must also die, burying your own will and judgment.

*

Renounce your own opinions, your own inclinations, all self-will; abandon yourselves, like dead men, to the will of your superiors. So long as you do not give yourselves, like corpses, into the hands of obedience, you can never taste the sweetness of the service of God.

Be as eager to break your own will as the thirsty stag is to drink of the refreshing waters.

Consider that day lost in which you do not sacrifice your own will by submitting it to that of another.

Frequently offer your will to God as a holocaust, and perfect contentment will be your reward. The more obedient you are, the more tranquil and indifferent you will be as to your employment. Holy obedience will be your true spouse, and you will love it in Jesus, that great King of obedient souls. Thus you will render your-selves more capable to serve the Church and our Congregation by means of your prayers. Jesus answers the prayer of obedient souls.

*

Our sweetest Jesus allowed Himself to be clothed and stripped, as it pleased His executioners; they bound Him and unbound Him, pushed Him from one side to the other, and the innocent Lamb submitted to all.

O sweet submission of Jesus, my sovereign God!

*

Continue to prepare yourself for everything as a meek lamb. Love to see your plans, though good, frustrated; a time will come when God will permit you fully to execute them.

*

Well, how goes it with you? Your heart would fain wing its flight to heaven, is it not so? But patience; you must wait till your

divine Spouse give you permission.

I learn that you suffer from
fever. I think that you would be
obedient even unto death, and you
know well that you have not yet
permission to leave your prison to
go to your home.

The poor father whom God
has given you for your director
would desire, if such were the
good pleasure of God, to be near
you, to wish your soul a safe
journey to heaven. And how could
you leave me now, when I need
you most? Let the work of the
Congregation be accomplished,
and afterwards I will allow you to
go in peace. You laugh at my folly?
I hope that the Divine Goodness
will compassionately hear this
foolish language.[1]

---

1   The religious to whom our saint thus wrote
     miraculously recovered his health.

The Passion and Mortification

I wish that I always had at hand a weeding tool to root up and entirely destroy the weed which continually springs up in my garden. You understand me; I mean that I endeavor to strip my soul of all that is not God.

*

St. Ignatius often said: "Ignatius, overcome thyself; Ignatius, overcome thyself."

Oh, what important advice! What a great point of perfection!

*

While the body is occupied at its labor, the soul can accomplish hers by thinking of God and loving Him. Thus, while we eat we can make some acts of the love of God, and so practice mortification; we may rise above all worldly interests, and escape the risk of becoming attached to created joys.

*

Shall we, in the spirit of mortification, abstain from drinking water? Yes, for the love of Jesus, Who was crucified and tormented with thirst on the cross, let us make this sacrifice.

*

St. Gregory the Great nourished himself with a dish of vegetables, as I have seen in an old engraving, in which his mother, St. Sylvia, is also represented; and in our times there is so much delicacy that we fear to impose upon ourselves even some moderate penances. St. Gregory, of a noble family, young, and of a delicate constitution, learned at the school of pious monks to content himself with a dish of vegetables sent him every day, as an alms, by his mother.

One such example ought to cover us with confusion.

The Passion and Humility

When God bestows His favors on you, keep your secret to yourself, according to the advice of the prophet Isaias: "My secret to myself, my secret to myself" (Isaias xxiv. 16), and seize every occasion to humble yourself.

*

God reveals His sublime secrets only to those who are humble of heart. Therefore entertain a sincere contempt of yourself; let it be your greatest desire to be regarded as an object worthy of contempt.

*

Arrived at this point of humility, abandon yourself to God, and He will illumine your soul with rays of divine light and cause you to lead a life of divine love—a holy life. These are some of the sublime effects which the Divine Majesty works in souls that are truly humble and render to God all the glory of His gifts. Read these sentiments attentively, but with a simple and open heart, after the example of the mother-pearl, which, having received the dew of heaven, closes itself and sinks to the bottom of the sea, there to form the precious pearl.

*

Humble yourself, resign yourself, and abandon yourself to God with entire confidence, always keeping in view your nothingness.

*

Act justly: keep what is your own—namely, your misery and frailty, capable of leading you to the commission of every crime; and leave to God that which belongs to Him, that is, every good.

*

We must fear that terrible beast, self-love; it is a serpent with seven heads which intrudes itself everywhere. There is nothing which frightens me more and puts me more on my guard against the impulses of my heart, lest they be prompted by it.

*

Ah! when shall we perfectly imitate our divine Redeemer, Who humbled Himself so much?

When shall we be sufficiently humble to glory in being the reproach of men, and the outcast of the people? (Ps. xxi. 7).

When shall it be our greatest pain to be esteemed and honored? Ah! when? In your charity beg of God to grant me this grace.

*

The deeper our humility, the higher will be our place in heaven. As Lucifer wished to raise himself to the highest place in heaven, and in punishment of his pride was cast into the depths of hell, so the soul that humbles herself most profoundly causes Satan to tremble and be confounded, and God exalts her to the glory of paradise.

*

Know that one grain of pride suffices to overthrow a mountain of holiness. Be humble, then, and endeavor to know yourself.

*

Humility and self-contempt are safe barriers against illusions.

*

When we see that prayer produces effects and desires befitting our state in life, there is no illusion to fear, provided that there results a fuller consciousness of our indigence, helplessness, and ignorance. Nothingness and Infinity: these two words comprise sublime perfection.

*

The grace of the Holy Ghost be ever with you. Amen.

I. I rejoice on account of the interior and exterior sufferings which you have to bear; I rejoice that you love them. You begin to be a disciple of Christ. It is true that yours are light crosses, and you ought to humble yourself by the consideration that they are nothing compared to those of the servants of God, and much less still when weighed in the balance of your Saviour's cross.

II. The prayer which humbles the soul, inflames her with love, and leads her to the practice of virtue, is not susceptible of illusion.

III. Fly, as a pest, that self-satisfaction which begets vanity and inspires you with an esteem of yourself; it comes from the devil.

Thank the Lord that you have the grace to recognize and reject it.

Humility of heart, self-contempt, recourse to the Sacred Heart of Jesus, the impregnable fortress to which we should ever fly for help—these are the chief means of guarding against illusion.

IV. Those sentiments which enlighten your mind and inflame your will ought, after what you have told me, to be suspected if they occasion you one particle of self-complacency. You should, therefore, banish those imaginations and place yourself in the presence of God, endeavoring with a lively faith to conceive a high idea of the Divine Majesty, that you may the more effectually humble yourself before Him. If the devil assail you, think of your sins and miseries; do not permit yourself to go further, but reflect on your own nothingness: you will thus baffle the ruses of the demon. Be faithful to this advice.

St. Francis Borgia, before applying himself to the sublime prayer of contemplation, was wont to spend two hours in meditating on his nothingness, etc.

True consolations and divine lights are always accompanied by a deep humility and such a knowledge of self and of God that we put ourselves under the feet of all. Moreover, they impart sometimes, though not always, clear understanding of heavenly things, along with peace, joy, the love of virtue, and a longing for grace.

*

Let us keep ourselves humble until God Himself will raise us up. Oh, when God wishes to raise up a soul, what gentle violence He uses! I say gentle, but it is so strong that the soul cannot resist it.

So let us remain, at first, in the presence of God in pure faith, with a deep sense of our nothingness, our sins and miseries afterwards; let us leave free to the soul the attractions of the Holy Ghost.

I may add that, though you think that you are rejoicing in your trials, you should not make any account of this disposition, because the devil could thereby easily fill you with vanity. It is better to fear and to distrust one's self, having in view only the will of God.

The world is full of snares; only humble souls can escape them. Do not trust yourself even though your prayer seems to produce good effects.

Be not judge in your own case, but distrust yourself, and adore the Father of lights in spirit and in truth. It is written: Happy the man who always fears!

To do well and to feel that we do nothing well is a sign of deep humility.

He is truly humble of heart who knows himself thoroughly and who knows God. May the Lord grant this grace to all men!

*

He shall be the greatest who will make himself the least. He that humbles himself the most profoundly shall be the most exalted; he shall have, the more easily, access to that wine-cellar, that royal hall, whence opens that secret sanctuary in which the soul communes face to face with her divine Spouse.

*

If any dust of imperfection cling to your heart, be not troubled, but consume it immediately in the fire of divine love, and, sorrowfully asking forgiveness, continue to live in peace.

*

From humility of heart proceed serenity of mind, gentleness of conduct, interior peace, and every good.

*

Imagine yourself a great nobleman, who, while at table with his friends, hears a loud knock at the door. He sends a servant to see who knocks, and learning that it is a beggar, grows angry at the beggar's impertinence, and dismisses him without an alms.

A little later another beggar knocks, but very humbly and modestly. The master then says to his servants: Let charity be given to this poor man who so humbly asks it. A third knocks, but so softly as to be scarcely heard. The master gives him a good sum of money.

Finally a poor leper comes, who has not the boldness to knock, and who throws himself on the ground near the door, and waits for the master to perceive him. The master, going out for a walk, observes the poor leper. "What are you doing here?" he inquires; "why do you not ask charity?"

"Ah! sir," replies the mendicant, "you are a great and good nobleman, and I am a poor and ragged man, covered with leprosy. I dare not even open my mouth." At these words the nobleman summons his steward, and says to him: "See that this poor man is cared for and clothed, and supply him with a generous annuity for the rest of his days."

It is thus that Our Lord acts towards us. The more we humble ourselves in His divine presence, the more will He enrich us with His graces. When we experience dryness, desolation, abandonment in prayer, we must greatly humble ourselves before God, acknowledging our demerits, imploring the aid of His grace, and suffering in humble resignation whatever affliction He may be pleased to send us.

*

The most simple means to be always favored with new gifts and graces, and to love God more and more, is to look with the eye of faith into the abyss of our nothingness, and, in the fear which this sight will inspire, to fly into the interior of the desert, in the abyss of the Divinity, wherein we let our nothingness disappear and passively receive divine inspirations.

Abandon yourself wholly to God; let the Divine Majesty accomplish this work in the secret of your soul. In this school of divine wisdom he is the most learned who becomes the most ignorant. In this school we understand without understanding, so to speak, for I cannot express myself. O holy ignorance, which causes all the wisdom and greatness of the world to vanish, and makes us learn, in the school of the Holy Spirit, the science and wisdom of the saints!

The Passion and the Holy Will of God

Be resigned to the will of God in all things; make frequent acts of submission; regard with the eye of faith all interior and exterior troubles as coming from God; do not think of the future—that is, of its misfortunes, its trials, and other occurrences which the imagination may conjure up, but dispel them in the will of God.

To continue my spiritual prescription: grind all your sufferings in the mill of patience and silence; knead them with the balm of Our Saviour's Passion into a little pill; swallow it with faith and love, and let the heat of charity digest it.

*

Lord, dispose of me as Thou willest; let me be tormented as much as Thou pleasest; I will never, on any account, separate myself from Thee. Do with me according to Thy good pleasure; I wish to draw nearer and nearer to Thee.

*

Lord, Thou fliest from me, but I will suffer this trial as long as it is Thy good pleasure. I will always be Thine; although Thou wilt fly from me, I will yet follow Thee.

*

In all your afflictions and interior desolations make frequent acts of total abandonment to the will of God. Recite the chaplet which St. Gertrude composed of these words only: *Fiat voluntas tua* —"May Thy will be done." At other times say, with sentiments of perfect conformity to the divine will, "Thou art just, O Lord! and all Thy judgments are just, and all

Thy ways are mercy, and truth, and judgment." (Tobias iii. 2).

*

One day the Lord let me see a huge bundle of crosses. At the same time He inspired me interiorly to plunge my own will, as a drop of water, into the immense ocean of the most amiable will of God. I did so, and in the twinkling of an eye all the crosses disappeared.

*

One of the clearest proofs that we love God is to seek only His good pleasure, to desire God alone: *Dilectus meus mihi et ego illi* —"My Beloved to me, and I to Him," (Cant. ii. 16), and to do His will as soon as we know it.

*

As the wax which we place near the fire assumes any form we wish to give it, so the loving soul ought to obey as soon as her Beloved has spoken.

*

May the will of God be our food, our center, our repose; therein we shall enjoy a peaceful sleep, which nothing can disturb.

*

May the will of God be done, may the Lord be forever blessed. I wish neither more nor less than the will and the good pleasure of God, whether in time or in eternity; I can will only that which my God wills.

*

In all annoying occurrences say, "May the holy and amiable will of God be done," or else, in the words of the Gospel, "I am come down from heaven, not to do My own will, but the will of Him that sent Me." (John vi. 38). "My meat is to do the will of Him that sent me." (John iv. 34).

*

He that resists the will of God can have neither rest nor peace. "Who hath resisted Him and hath had peace?" (Job ix. 4).

In the trials that God sends us we must bow our head in submission, because, if He intended to give us one stroke, and we raise our head in rebellion, He will give us ten of them; whereas, if He designed to give us ten strokes, and we bow our heard in submission, He will scarcely inflict one.

*

Never consider the instrument of your trials; try to realize that Jesus presents them to you with His own hand.

*

If, on going to the garden to pluck some fruits, you were surprised by a heavy rain, what would you do? You would seek shelter under the shed, would you not? So when sorrow, bitterness, tribulation, rain down upon you, you must seek a refuge in the safe asylum of the will of God, and you shall not be troubled.

*

When shall we be dead to all things that we may live for God? Ah! yes, when will that time arrive? O precious death! more desirable than life; death which, through love, transforms us into God!

St. John Chrysostom said: *Silentium, quod lutem praebet figulo, idem ipse praebe conditori tuo.* Oh, what a sentence! He would say, "As the clay is silent in the hands of the potter, so do you be silent in the hands of your Creator." The clay remains silent whether the potter forms it into a vessel of honor or of ignominy, whether he breaks it or flings it among the rubbish; it is content to be cast aside or to be placed in an art gallery. Impress this lesson on your memory.

*

Even the holiest desires, whether they refer to the salvation of souls or the needs of the Church, which are very great, should be consumed in the fire of the love of God, whence they proceed, and await God's time for their fulfillment. Meanwhile cultivate one only desire, the most perfect of all; that is, to please God more and more, and to nourish yourself with His will.

*

Sustain yourself with the holy will of God; drink of the chalice of Jesus with closed eyes, caring not what its contents may be; it suffices to know that this chalice is offered to you by the sweet Jesus.

*

Say frequently and from your heart, "O holy will of God, I love thee; the food of my Jesus was to do the will of the eternal Father; it shall be my food also ever to do His will."

Do not let the devil frighten you. Keep yourself hidden in God, and nothing can hurt you.

Never neglect prayer. Be strong and constant. Courage! God wishes to make a saint of you. May Jesus bless you!

*

The divine will is a balm which heals every wound. We should caress it and love it in adversity as well as in prosperity.

We ought to imitate the gardeners and the vine-dressers; when a storm breaks out they retire to the shed, and remain there until the storm has passed. So, in the midst of the tempests with which we are threatened on account of our sins and those of the world, we should retire under the golden tent of the divine will, rejoicing that the good pleasure of the Sovereign Master is being accomplished in all things.

*

I wish neither life nor death, but only that which God wills.

*

Offer to the eternal Father the precious blood of His only Son in propitiation for my ingratitude, and to obtain for me the grace to do His will. If this work be not for His glory, may He bring it to naught, and grant me time and an asylum, in order to do penance for and weep over my sins.

The Passion and Confidence in God

In every holy work arm yourself with confidence in God; let no obstacles frighten you. God will enable you to do wonders. Be, then, generous and courageous. Put your shoulder to the wheel with humility and purity of intention, having in view only the glory of God. Thank Him for having chosen you as an instrument of His glory, and, humbling yourself in His presence, cry out, "I am as nothing before Thee." (Ps. Xxxviii. 6).

*

Have great diffidence of yourself. "Without Me," your Saviour tells you, "you can do nothing." (John xv. 5). And the apostle St. James: "Every perfect gift is from above." (James i. 17).

*

Beginners in the service of God sometimes lose confidence when they fall into any fault. When you feel so unworthy a sentiment rising within you, you must lift your heart to God and consider that all your faults, compared with divine goodness, are less than a bit of oakum thrown into a sea of fire.

*

Suppose that the whole horizon, as far as you can see from this mountain, were a sea of fire; if we cast into it a bit of oakum, it will disappear in an instant. So, when you have committed a fault, humble yourself before God, and cast your fault into the infinite ocean of charity, and at once it will be effaced from your soul; at the same time all distrust will disappear.

*

Where is the father who, beholding a beloved son in his arms, would let him fall to the earth? And if an earthly father would not act thus, much less would a God of infinite love. we must have courage in His service.

*

Renew your confidence by a glance at the cross. See that precious blood, those mortal wounds, those hands which have made heaven and earth are still outstretched to poor, repentant sinners who humbly sigh for the embrace of Jesus.

*

If any one thought to sweeten the vast waters of the sea with one drop of fresh water, would he not be justly regarded as a fool? So also the man who thinks or hopes to do any good without the help of God grievously deceives himself. If he claims any

good as his own, God will not fail
to humble and confound him; such
a man could never become the
Lord's instrument, nor accomplish
great things for His glory.

*

Science without true humility only inflates; but humility,
joined to prayer and confidence in
God and the necessary fund of
knowledge, moves God, so to
speak, to work wonders for the
conversion of souls the conversion
of sinners is a work all divine.

*

"Every plant that My
heavenly Father hath not planted
shall be rooted up." (Matt. xv. 13).

*

I have never worried about
our temporal affairs, and I have
seen by experience that God has
always provided for us. When we
were two, Providence provided
enough for two; for four when we

were four; and when our number increased the needs of all were supplied, thus verifying the divine promise: "Seek ye first the kingdom of God, and His justice, and all these things shall be added unto you." (Matt. vi. 33). "Be not solicitous for your life, what you shall eat, nor for your body, what you shall put on." (Matt. vi. 25).

*

The vessel is launched on the sea, without sail or oar, but she is guided by the captain, who will conduct her safely to port. She is battered by wind and tempest, but this displays only the better the capability and wisdom of her captain. May Jesus Christ ever reign in our hearts, Who hath given us the strength to suffer all things for His love.

*

In the works of God progress is really the greatest when

obstacles seem to crowd thick and fast.

Pray for us that Our Lord may enable us to triumph over our enemies so terribly arrayed against us.

*

Self-contempt and perfect union with the divine will: these are the main points of the Christian life.

The Passion and Sufferings

One day the Lord caused me to hear these words at the foot of the tabernacle: "My son, he who embraces Me embraces thorns." Oh, what a grace! Oh, what a gift!

*

Through the divine operation which the Infinite Goodness has effected in your soul you call that sweet which is truly very sweet; but there will come a time when you will take your nourishment on the cross, feeding only on that which was your Saviour's food.

Nourish your soul generously, and sleep well, because this kind of food requires a prolonged sleep in interior solitude.

*

Meditation on Jesus Christ crucified is a precious balm which sweetens all pains.

*

What an honor God confers on us, when He calls us to travel the same road as His divine Son!

*

Make great account of your precious trials, both interior and exterior; it is thus that the garden of Jesus is adorned with flowers, that is, with acts of virtue.

*

The more deeply the cross penetrates, the better; the more deprived suffering is of consolation the purer it will be; the more creatures oppose us, the more closely shall we be united to God.

*

In the sweetness and delight of the soul there is always danger of the devil playing a wicked trick on us.

*

He who has not suffered and overcome some fierce temptation is unworthy of divine contemplation.

*

Adversities teach us and aid us to hold the just balance.

*

In consolations a child may be brave, but it is in serious tribulations that we distinguish the strong from the effeminate soul.

*

Believe me, afflictions, fears, desolations, dryness, abandonment, temptations, and other persecutions make an excellent broom, which sweeps from your soul all the dust of hidden imperfections.

*

To labor, to suffer, to be silent, to complain not, to bear no resentment—these are the maxims of the saints, the maxims of high perfection.

*

Have you ever noticed rocks in the sea, beaten by the tempest? A furious wave dashes against the rock, another and yet another does likewise, yet the rock is unmoved. But look at it after the storm has subsided, and you will see that the flood has but served to wash and purify it of the defilement it had contracted during the calm.

Hereafter I wish you to be as a rock. A wave dashes against you? Silence! It assails you ten, a hundred, a thousand times? Silence! Say, at most, in the midst of the storm, "My Father, my Father, I am all Thine! O dear, O sweet will of God, I adore Thee!"

*

The statue must be chiselled with very sharp tools before it is fit to be placed in the grand gallery.

*

The holy gospel tells us that unless the grain of wheat, falling into the ground, die, itself remaineth alone, and does not bear fruit. The poor grain thus sown, how much must it not suffer to die and fructify! It must endure rain, snow, wind, and sun. The soul is a seed that God sows in the field of holy Church; to fructify, it must die by dint of pain, contradiction, and persecution.

*

All the little trials of body and mind are the first steps of that sublime and holy ladder which is mounted by great and generous souls. Step by step they climb to the top, on which is found pure suffering devoid of all heavenly and earthly consolation.

If they be faithful and seek no satisfaction in creatures, they pass from pure suffering to the pure love of God. But the fortunate souls who succeed thus far are very few.

Ah! picture a soul who has been favored with heavenly consolations finding herself afterwards long despoiled of all happiness. Imagine her, arrived at the point of believing herself forsaken by God, believing that God has no longer any regard for her, that He is incensed at her. The state of that soul is such that she sees evil in all she does. Ah! I cannot express myself as I would. Let it suffice for you to know that, in this state, the soul almost suffers the torments of hell—a trial surpassing every other. But if the soul will faithfully brave it, oh, what treasures she gains! The tempest will finally cease, and the soul will receive the sweet embraces of Jesus, her true friend. God then treats her as His spouse;

there is then contracted between God and this favored soul a holy alliance of love.

Oh, what treasure! As for you, you are not yet on the first step of that golden ladder. However, I have written to you in this vein that you may not be frightened when God will be pleased to require of you some degree of pure suffering without consolation; then, more than ever, be faithful to God, and do not abandon your ordinary exercises.

*

Sufferings are the richest presents that the Divine Majesty bestows on you.

God wills that, like precious stones, you be firmly set in the golden ring of charity. He wills that you be so many victims, so many holocausts, sacrificed to the glory of the Most High in the sacred fire of suffering. He wills that through this sacrifice you may continually diffuse the good odor of virtues.

*

The soul that God would draw by means of prayer to a very close union with Himself ought, even in prayer, to pass by the way of suffering, of suffering divested of all consolation, the soul, in a certain sense, knowing not where she is; nevertheless, she understands, by the light infused into her from above, that she is always in the arms of her heavenly Spouse, sustained with the milk of His divine love.

*

I wish that all men could understand the great favor that God grants them when, in His goodness, He sends them suffering, and especially suffering devoid of all consolation; for then the soul, like gold which is purified in the fiery crucible, is cleansed, made beautiful, detached from earthly things, and united to the Sovereign Good, without even being conscious of it.

*

How happy you will be if you are faithful in combating and overcoming your natural inclinations, and do not allow yourself to be overcome by them, fixing your gaze on the face of Jesus, Who, as a special favor, invites you to follow Him!

The Passion and the Trials of the Soul

Remember that true holiness is accompanied by pains and tribulations from within and without, by attacks of visible and invisible enemies, by trials of body and mind, by desolations and prolonged aridities; "and all that will live godly in Christ Jesus shall suffer persecution," (2 Tim. iii. 12) —that is to say, all sorts of trials from demons, from men, and from our rebellious flesh.

*

Be generous and remember that you ought to walk in the footsteps of your Redeemer.

*

We must not serve God for the sake of His consolations, but because He is worthy of being served.

God usually deprives His servants, for a time, of all consolation, that they may learn to serve Him through pure love, and become truly faithful servants. He deprives them of spiritual delights, even on the most solemn occasions, to test their faith and fidelity.

Sursum corda, then; let us lift up our hearts and generously serve our great God and Our Lord Jesus in faith and pure love. Amen.

*

My trials are great! However, "although God should kill me, I will trust in Him." (Job xiii. 15). What ought a poor shipwrecked person do when in the midst of furious billows and on the point of being engulfed? I have no other resource left but to turn my eyes to the Lord.

I find myself threatened by new combats... Storms succeed

each other, darkness increases, fears do not vanish, demons harass me, men slander me, combats within, fears without, darkness, coldness, tepidity, desolation. What can one do in the midst of so many dangers? Ah! death is more desirable than life. Yes, if such is the will of God, may the door of a blessed eternity open to me! I know not which way to turn; however, I have faith and confidence that God will accomplish His work in a wonderful way.

*

Everybody is against us. I rejoice in this, for God will be more favorable to us...If we be faithful, God will not fail us.

*

One day, when the weather was extremely cold, I wished to make a fire. I went to the woods to pick up some dry branches, which had been exposed to the air for a long time. In a moment I had a big fire. Why? Because for a long time the wood had been exposed to the cold, the frost, the wind, and the sun, and had thus lost its dampness. So it is with us: if we wish our hearts to become inflamed with divine love, we must permit ourselves to be purified by suffering, humbly and resignedly, temptations, trials, persecutions, tribulations. Oh! being then well cleansed, divine love will possess us.

*

How happy is the soul who detaches herself from all pleasure, from all sentiment, from all self-opinionatedness! You will realize this happiness if you put all your satisfaction in the cross of Jesus; that is, if you die on the cross of your Saviour to all that is not God.

As for the aversion that people express for you, their

mockeries, their derisions, and so forth, you should receive them with gratitude to God, for as oil is consumed by the flame, so ought charity consume its victim.

*

If you desire an efficacious remedy for trouble and inquietude of soul, invoke the holy name of Jesus.

One time I was stopping near the sea, engaged at a mission. In compliance with their request, I joined the fishermen in a fishing expedition. As the sea was very rough, they threw into it, from time to time, some drops of oil, and the waters became calm immediately, so that they had no trouble in catching the fish. When our mind is agitated as the sea during a storm, let us restore its calm by invoking the name of Jesus, of Whom it is said in the

Canticle of Canticles "Thy name is as oil poured out." (Cant. i. 2).

*

Your soul needs a brief winter. The winter purifies the air and the earth of foul vapors; it even invigorates the human body. If it strips the trees of their leaves, it is only to the end that they take deeper roots. The spring comes afterwards, and clothes them again with verdure and blossoms.

Each degree of prayer presupposes a purification. Be faithful in all your exercises of piety and virtue; be always resigned; be satisfied, in the superior part of your soul, to taste, without relish, the contentment of doing God's will. Thus after the winter the spring will come, with its flowers, and you will hear the voice of the turtle in this land. (Cant. ii. 12).

*

In all your trials, arm yourself with faith, confidence in God, and deep humility of heart. Reiterate your commands to Satan; order him, in the name of Jesus Christ, to depart and betake himself to the place that God, on account of his pride, has assigned for him. Fear nothing.

*

Temptations are excellent signs; and the pain they occasion you is as a fire which will purify you and prepare you better and better for union with God.

*

When you feel an impulse of passion or anger rising within yourself, then is the moment for silence. Jesus was silent in the midst of His trials. O sacred silence, how rich thou art in virtues! O holy silence! thou art the golden key which unlocks the grand treasury of virtues!

*

God created the fish dumb because they are to live in the waters. By this He teaches us that he who lives amid the tempests of this world ought to be mute, as if he had no tongue, never complaining or justifying himself.

*

God, in permitting you to have this trial, wishes you to die mystically to all but Himself. He wishes you to consider yourself as dead; to have, as it were, neither tongue, nor eyes, nor ears. As you crush under your foot the crawling worm, so let yourself be trampled upon by everybody; let yourself be the despised and the outcast of the people, as if you were dead and buried.

*

I learn with joy that your confessor treats you rigorously, that he is hard and severe. Oh, what an excellent friend he is to you! It is now that God will put the last touch to the statue in order to embellish it and render it worthy of heaven; therefore He permits him, who ought to encourage you, to use the finest and sharpest tools. Oh, what a noble work! Beg God not to deprive you of that instrument until the work that He wishes to effect in you be accomplished. Do not be troubled by the annoyances and fears that your confessor occasions you. Listen to him with deep humility, simplicity, and silence.

When he dismisses you, retire in peace and at once send up some tender sighs to God: "O Father! O my good Father!" Tell Him of the trouble, the anguish, and the inquietude that your confessor's words give you. Immediately your soul will be sweetly drawn into the depths of that divine solitude where the soul is absorbed in God. Your anguish, your fears, your scruples, will be consumed in the furnace of divine love. Repose there, and if your divine Spouse invite you to sleep, sleep in peace, and do not awaken without His permission. This holy sleep is a heritage which our heavenly Father gives to His well-loved children: it is a sleep of faith and love wherein we learn the science of the saints, and during which the bitterness of adversities is dissipated.

*

You do wrong to complain of your crosses and sufferings. Believe me, you know not what it is to suffer.

God preserve you from suffering even one day what has been endured by a certain soul, whose name I must not disclose!

In my opinion, you ought not lay so much stress on your little trials, your spiritual darkness and dryness. When we truly and sincerely love God, we regard as little that which we suffer for our divine Lover.

If you believe that you suffer much, it is an evidence that you have very little love for your Saviour.

*

The proof that we love is to suffer much for the Beloved, and to esteem all we suffer as nothing.

*

I exhort you to hide your treasure as well as you can. You understand of what treasure I speak; it is your precious sufferings.

The pearl is formed in the shell; but the shell, which has received the dew of heaven, closes itself and sinks to the bottom of the sea, where it engenders the precious pearl. Understand me well. The pearl of genuine virtue is engendered in the depths of the sea of suffering and humility. Thence we pass into the immense ocean of uncreated love and allow ourselves to be swallowed up in its waters.

Put in practice these precious words: suffer, be silent. By doing so, you will become in a short time holy and perfect.

*

Souls who aspire to a sublime union with God by contemplation usually suffer interior purgations in one way or another.

*

God's ways are incomprehensible. He uses very sharp files, which penetrate the heart and remove the rust. His files are all spiritual.

*

There are some trials which are more bitter, so to say, than hell itself. These trials, being pure, devoid of all interior and exterior consolation, prepare the soul admirably for union with God. When God permits a soul to be in this state of purgation, it is a sign that she is making progress. She must, however, observe whether she has a secret esteem of her state —this would be pernicious—see whether her prayer leave her fully conscious of her own nothingness and lead her to extol the divine mercy.

*

God sends such purgations to you, directors of consciences, that you may acquire the science of the saints and the art of directing souls. You will suffer also in another way. Love will be your executioner. Let it do its work; it knows how. In this martyrdom we have need of extraordinary grace and strength; but God will bestow it. Without this divine help it would be impossible to bear up.

*

This repugnance which you feel for riches is an excellent sign. God thus proves your fidelity, so that at each moment you may acquire new joys and new pearls for the embellishment of your crown.

*

Fancy a sculptor who sends for a piece of wood which he wishes to form into a fine statue. The wood-choppers carry to his shop a rough and shapeless log. The sculptor begins to smooth it down, using first the hatchet, then the saw, afterwards the plane, and finally the chisel. What does the wood do? Does it make any resistance? No, it allows itself to be worked upon until it becomes a beautiful statue. Thus acts the Divine Artist. With a view of freeing the soul from her imperfections and, as it were, of polishing her, He permits the demons to torment her by temptations, and then He tries her by means of aridities and desolations. If she bears these trials with patience and longanimity, she perfects herself and becomes a very beautiful statue, worthy of a place in the art gallery of heaven.

The Passion and Sickness

Sickness is a great grace of God; it teaches us what we are; in it we recognize the patient, humble, and mortified man. When sickness weakens and mortifies the body, the soul is better disposed to raise herself up to God.

*

As regards your bodily health, obey the orders of the physician. Tell him sincerely what you suffer, in modest, clear, and concise language; after having said all that is necessary, be silent and let him act. Do not refuse remedies, but take them in the loving chalice of Jesus, with a pleasant countenance.

Be grateful to the person who nurses you; take whatever she offers you. In brief, act as a child in the arms of its mother. Remain in

your bed as on the cross. Jesus
prayed for three hours on the
cross, and His was a truly crucified
prayer, with no comfort from
within or without. O God! what a
grand lesson! Beg God to imprint it
on your heart. Oh, what a subject
for meditation!

*

There could not be a surer
sign of God's love for you that this
pain which He has sent you.
Adore the divine will. You were in
good health when you were in the
world, but you were not then as
dear to God as you are now. He
loves you as a daughter, as a
cherished spouse: this is why He
treats you so generously. Long
illnesses are the greatest favors
that God confers on souls whom
He loves most...Repose peacefully
in the arms of your heavenly
Spouse, Who loves you much;
hold yourself on the cross of

sickness as tranquilly and silently as is possible. If the cause of your illness be the wound of divine love which embalms your soul, it is well if you die under such a stroke: yours will be a death more precious than life.

*

The best way to acquire that peace which is born of the love of God, the inexhaustible Source of all virtues, is to accept all tribulations, whether spiritual or temporal, as coming directly from the paternal hand of God; to look upon all unpleasant events as very costly gifts presented to us by our heavenly Father; to repeat often the sacred words of Our Saviour: "Yea Father, for so hath it seemed good in Thy sight." (Matt. xi. 26).

From all eternity the Lord has judged it fitting, and willed it, that you should suffer those bodily ailments, those assaults of Satan,

and those persecutions from men.
Look upon them with the eye of
faith, and adore the good pleasure
of God by pious ejaculations.

*

Beholding with the eye of
faith bitterness, persecutions, and
sufferings of soul or body—
beholding them, I say, with the eye
of faith, as so many jewels sent us
by divine love, they are no longer
bitter, but become most sweet and
pleasing.

*

Sickness is a good discipline
and a rough hair-cloth. Oh, how
pleasing to God are the disciplines
which He sends us!

The Passion and Interior Solitude

Examine yourself well, in order to ascertain whether God alone lives in you. By self-examination you will know whether you perform all your actions for the love of God, and unite them to those of Our Lord Jesus Christ, Who is our way, our truth, and our life. Truly, you are dead, and your life is hidden in God with Christ. Since you are dead to everything that is not God, keep yourself perfectly detached from every creature. God loves childlike souls. He teaches them that wisdom which He has concealed from the wise and prudent of the world. (Matt. xi. 25).

Never stray away from the sacred wounds of Jesus. Let the sufferings of your Divine Redeemer be deeply impressed on your heart, and be assured that He, the Good Shepherd, will conduct you as a cherished lamb to His divine fold. And what is the fold of this amiable Shepherd? It is the bosom of His heavenly Father.

*

If you wish to preserve or acquire the gift of prayer, keep yourself recollected by making, even in the midst of your occupations, frequent aspirations to God.

Watch over all your senses, and particularly over your eyes. By guarding the eyes, interior recollection may be acquired; for when we are at the window, or at the door, we may see what is going on outside, but not what is passing within; whereas, if we direct our attention to the interior of the house, we know nothing of what is passing without.

*

When you find yourself lost in interior solitude, and when you would rest more peacefully on the bosom of your heavenly Father, lament as a child and tell Him of the demon's wickedness towards you. He knows it already, but He wishes you to complain with the simplicity of a child. Tell Him, but with deep humility, not to allow the demon to molest you any longer.

*

When the soul finds herself in the sacred silence of faith and love, and feels an interior impulse to pray for the wants of the Church, or of the world, for some special or general intention, she should do so immediately; but this interior movement ceasing, she ought to repose again in God. If this repose transform itself into the sleep of love and faith, so much the better. The Divine Goodness, I hope, will make you understand this language if you be very humble and retain a full sense of your nothingness.

*

Fly from the world, and commence by trampling under your feet all human respect. Do not blush to be a servant of Christ. Regard this world with the same horror that the sight of a criminal suspended from a gibbet would awaken in you. Know that the atmosphere of the world is polluted with the foul odor of thousands of sins that are constantly committed, and which can be washed away only by tears of blood.

*

Why should we be attached to this world, where we can breathe only air poisoned by so many crimes?

I beg you to close to creatures the door of your heart, and keep yourself shut up in the interior of your soul, that you may commune peacefully with your Beloved.

We should hold only so much intercourse with creatures as charity and social etiquette demand, and no more.

*

The oratory and the cell constitute the earthly paradise of the true servants of God.

*

You should find delight only in three places—namely, in the oratory, in the cell, and in the interior temple of your soul, which is the principal one.

*

Parlors are the ruin of monasteries.

*

The moment has come for you to keep yourself in interior solitude, and to repose peacefully on the bosom of God. There you will learn to become a saint.

The Passion and Perfect Detachment

Do not fail to practice true poverty of spirit, by living in complete detachment from all sensible consolation, interior as well as exterior, so as not to fall into the vice of spiritual gluttony.

*

We must become detached from self-gratification, our own opinions and sentiments, that we may escape the dangers of a spiritual curiosity, and practice true poverty of spirit.

*

You should not pay so much attention to or dwell on certain gifts, but rather go to the Divine Source whence they proceed.

*

Pay no attention to sensible consolations; make of them a

sacrifice to God, and never set your heart on them.

*

The trees which are planted on the river's bank absorb the moisture without changing their place; so, when the soul receives the impress of divine favors, she ought to remain immovably fixed in God, the Supreme Giver, because there is great danger of illusion in dwelling on the gifts and the sweetness thereof.

*

The gifts of God leave in the humble soul a deep knowledge of her own insufficiency, a love of contempt, a fervor in the practice of virtue; they move her to keep her secret from all creatures except the spiritual father whom God gives her as her director.

*

The soul should not dwell on the gifts, but on the Giver.

*

When we go into the garden, it is not to gather the leaves, but the fruits; so in the sacred garden of prayer we ought not to amuse ourselves with the leaves of sentiment and sensible consolation, but rather reap the fruits of the virtues of Jesus.

*

If you desire God to work wonders in your soul, you ought to keep yourself as much as is possible detached from all created things, in true poverty of spirit, and in perfect interior solitude. O sacred desert in which the soul learns the science of the saints, like Moses in the solitude of Mount Horeb!

The Passion and the Sacred Heart of Jesus

Let your heart consume itself more and more in the sanctuary of the Heart of Jesus, and let the ashes of the victim fall into the boundless ocean of divine charity.

*

The moment has come when you should more than ever die to all that is not God, that you may the more lovingly commune with Him alone. Let your life be as hidden as possible. Lock yourself up in the great sanctuary of the divine Heart, for there the soul is nourished by her divine Spouse with that wine which strengthens, vivifies, inflames the soul, and causes her to take flight to the contemplation of the supreme Monarch; it is in that sanctuary that the soul learns the science of the saints, which is taught only to the humble.

*

In the Heart of Jesus be constantly recollected; it is not necessary that you should feel and taste the divine presence, but it is all-important that you keep yourself in that presence by pure faith, devoid of all self-satisfaction.

*

When you attain true humility of heart and self-contempt ask leave of Jesus to enter His divine Heart, and you will at once obtain it. Place yourself as a victim on that altar, where the fire of divine love is ever burning. Let this sacred flame burn you to the marrow of your bones; then, if the breath of the Holy Spirit raise you to the contemplation of the divine mysteries, leave to your soul the liberty of losing herself in this holy

contemplation. Oh, how pleasing
to God is this practice!

*

O Jesus, my Sovereign Good,
when Thou wert scourged, what
were the sentiments of Thy most
holy Heart! O dear Spouse of my
soul, how greatly did the sight of
my sins and my ingratitude afflict
Thee! O my Love! would that I
could die for Thee!

The Passion and Peace of Heart

Rest tranquilly in the loving Heart of our dear Saviour; do not lose peace, even though the world turn upside down.

*

One of the best proofs that we advance in virtue is to be at peace amid the attacks and the contradictions of creatures. Be firm on this point, and despise all the assaults of hell. More than ever show your fidelity to God by reposing on the cross with equanimity of spirit, and even exteriorly be calm and serene, without murmur or complaint. Drink of the chalice which Jesus Himself offers you; if it be bitter to the palate, it is sweet to the heart.

*

Nothing but sin can separate us from God. You do not wish to sin; therefore preserve your heart in peace, and have it constantly turned towards heaven.

*

Keep interior peace at every cost; pay no attention to fears or scruples. Experience will teach you that those vain fears of sin, etc., which I call veritable follies, ought to disappear in the fire of love.

I beg of you to appreciate the great favor which is accorded you in being always of a contrite and humble heart.

*

Make of your fears and other silly scruples a bundle, and throw it into the fire of divine charity, which will at once consume it; then keep yourself in interior solitude, and rest on the bosom of your heavenly Father.

*

Be very careful to retain peace of heart, because Satan casts his lines in troubled waters.

*

The notion that you commit sin in everything you do is a wicked suggestion of the devil; it is not true.

Humble yourself before God; lose yourself in the very depths of that sacred desert of which I have spoken to you; be absorbed by the Sovereign Good, consumed by the sacred fire of love. Believe me, this divine fire will dissipate all the dust and mist of scruples, and your soul will become purer and more beautiful in the eyes of your heavenly Spouse.

Keep yourself in a silence of faith and love, as a victim offered to the glory of God, and courageously despise scruples.

The merciful visits with which your Saviour favors you are

not liable to illusion; they cause you to know how much He loves you, and that your scruples are an artifice of the demon.

*

When you are annoyed by scruples, say: "Yes, my Jesus, yes, I firmly trust that Thou hast pardoned me. My confessions have been well made, since my spiritual father has told me so. I believe Thy minister, and not the devil, who seeks to ruin me and to deprive me of peace of heart. So, my soul, courage! God has pardoned thee; trust in Him. O my God, my Father! I hope in Thee, I love Thee. Infernal spirit, begone from me! No more scruples, no more doubts, no more fears! May the love of my Jesus live in me! May the love of Jesus reign forever!"

The Passion and Illusions

There are people who fancy they have visions. Such fancies are dangerous, for through them the devil seeks to deceive; he does not proceed hurriedly, but quietly, the better to ensnare poor, foolish heads. Those visions, elevations, and lights are seldom genuine. Hence, says a great saint, "it is always best to reject them, to distrust them, particularly in the case of women, whose imagination is most vivid." In acting thus, we act well, because, if they come from God, they will not fail to produce their effect, even though we ignore them; and if they come from the devil, which is more probable, we guard ourselves, in rejecting them, against illusion.

*

Those locutions are very dangerous, and I cannot approve of them. I shall tell you the reason, founded on the little experience which God has given me. What necessity is there that God should reveal to a novice that He desires from the novices more fervor in their Communions? Is it, perchance, that their master, with the aid of the lights that God has given him for his office, does not know it himself? And again: does he not know that God is greatly offended chiefly by sacrileges? You see that this locution is not necessary. God makes revelations only in view of His glory and the needs of holy Church; and as we can learn these things from holy books, from the experience God gives us, and, principally, by the light He gives those that hold offices, there is no reason for desiring to learn by locutions.

*

When God speaks to souls by lights or impressions, in an angelic manner, without articulated words, His communications are sublime, being purely intellectual. In this case God speaks with great majesty, and His word produces wonderful effects.

When locutions are accompanied by interior articulated words, and they are spoken by God, or, as is more usually the case, by an angel speaking in the name of his sovereign Master, then also the words are sublime and majestic; they make a marvelous impression, and raise the soul to God.

Of a hundred, and perhaps a thousand, of these articulated locutions, there is hardly one genuine. It is difficult, even for spiritual masters, to discern the true from the false, those of the

Spirit of truth from those of the devil, who knows so well how to feign effects like in appearance to those of the Spirit of God. Therefore it is best to enjoin on him who has them to drive them away, to humble himself before God, and to protest that faith, with the Scriptures and the advice of his spiritual father, who speaks in God's name, are sufficient for him. Thus he glorifies God in distrusting himself, in humbling himself, in esteeming himself unworthy of such favors, and is thereby freed from illusion.

*

The gifts of God produce a profound knowledge of His infinite majesty, a deep sense of our own nothingness, a sincere detachment from all created things, a great love for the cross and sufferings, a particular inclination for prayer, and an exact obedience in everything that is not sin.

On the contrary, if locutions proceed from the devil, they seem at first to inspire devotion, but the sentiment does not last: they give rise to a secret presumption and self-esteem; they are followed sooner or later by inquietude of mind and the awakening of the passions.

The Passion and the Practices of a Christian Life

I am going to give you some spiritual advice, that you may advance, every day, in the love of God.

In the first place, observe with perfect exactitude the holy law of God. Have a filial fear of God, so worthy of love, Who has created and redeemed us. Know that the more tenderly a son loves his father, the more he fears to offend him. This holy fear will be a curb which will prevent you from committing sin. Love God with an ardent love; place in Him a childlike confidence; let all your words, all your actions, your pains, your sighs, and your tears, be a holocaust offered to His holy love.

To preserve this love, frequent the sacraments. Do not approach the altar but to inflame your soul more and more with divine love.

I say nothing to you of preparation; you will do your best, I think; remember that to receive Holy Communion is to perform the holiest action.

Often go to the church to adore the Blessed Sacrament, and visit with fervent piety the altar of the Blessed Virgin. Do not pass one day without devoting a half hour, or at least a quarter of an hour, to meditation on the sorrowful Passion of your Saviour. Have a continual remembrance of the agonies of your Crucified Love, and know that the greatest saints, who now, in heaven, triumph in holy love, arrived at perfection in this way. Cultivate a tender devotion to the dolors of Mary, to her Immaculate Conception, to your guardian angel, to your patron saints, and the holy apostles.

Often say ejaculatory prayers, but always with your whole heart. I will point out some to you: "Ah! my God, would that I never offended Thee! Ah! my Sovereign Good, wound, wound my heart with Thy holy love! He that loves Thee not, O my God! knows Thee not! When will my soul be filled with Thy divine charity!"

*

In your pains and trials say: "May Thy holy will be done, O my God! Welcome, ye afflictions! Beloved sufferings, I press you to my heart! Ah! dear hand of my God, I bless Thee! Blessed be the holy rod that strikes me with so much love! Ah! tender Father, it is good for me to be humbled!"

You can make these ejaculations while walking or working, and even when in company with others; for though you be externally engaged with others, your heart is free, and through your heart you can benefit your soul, even in the midst of the most serious occupations.

Every day read a pious book, and avoid bad company as you would Satan. Obey with the greatest exactitude. Obedience is a celestial pearl. Jesus Himself, through obedience, laid down His most holy life on the hard wood of the cross. Charitably compassionate the poor. Be just to all. Humble yourself before everybody, for the love of God.

Finally, I pray you, remember always the holy commandment of love that Christ gave to His disciples before going to death: "A new commandment I give unto you: That you love one another, as I have loved you, that you also love one another." (John xiii. 34). Ah, what sweet language! Remember that you will never please God if you do not love one another. Let there never be any dissension among you, and if an angry word should escape you, become gentle immediately, be silent, and do not allow anger to control your heart.

I place you in the sacred wounds of Jesus, under the protection of Our Lady of Sorrows; yes, I place you there. I implore the holy Virgin to bathe your heart in her sorrowful tears, that she may impress on it a continual remembrance of the dolorous Passion of her Son, and of her own dolors. I implore her to obtain for you perseverance in divine love, and strength and resignation in suffering. Take, then, for your glorious protectress, Our Lady of Sorrows, and never cease to meditate on the Passion of Christ. May God, in His mercy, bless you! Ask Him to bless me also. *Deo Gratias et Mariae semper Virgini!*

The Passion and the Rule of Life

I. In the morning, immediately after rising, make about a quarter of an hour's mental prayer, and then a spiritual communion.

II. Hear Mass, or should you be prevented, bear the disappointment with patience.

III. Work until dinner in holy silence, having your mind united to God; when spoken to, however, reply with sweetness, good grace, and charity.

IV. A half hour before dinner read a little, and, if you can, remain recollected before your crucifix for about fifteen minutes.

V. Dine in peace, observing a prudent mortification.

VI. After dinner take some recreation in company with others, always full of charity and amiability.

VII. Work until five o'clock or a little later, the mind being always united to God; then prepare for mental prayer and apply yourself to it for an hour.

VIII. Have supper, then a little recreation, retire, examine your conscience, do some spiritual reading, say your night-prayer, and go to bed.

I recommend to you the presence of God, the Source of all good. May God give you His blessing![2]

---

2   St. Paul of the Cross marked out this rule of life for a young person of good family. Its suavity, discretion, liberty of spirit, and, at the same time, its austerity, all point to the school of St. Francis de Sales.

Summary of Christian Perfection

I. Passion of Jesus Christ.

The Passion of Our Lord Jesus Christ is the shortest way to perfection.

The life of Christ was but a continuous cross.

God confers a great honor on us when He calls us to walk the same path as His only Son. If you correspond to the designs of God, He will make a saint of you.

Be generous, and remember that we ought to walk in the footsteps of Jesus crucified.

The servant of God who is not crucified with Jesus Christ, what is he?

He is unworthy of divine contemplation who has not fought and conquered some great temptation.

God has suffered much for me; ought I not suffer something for Him?

II. The Eucharist.

Holy Communion is the most efficacious means of uniting the soul to God.

The best preparation for the divine banquet is to keep ourselves well purified, and to watch over our tongue, which is the first member that touches the sacred Host.

On the day that we receive Holy Communion we should endeavor to keep our hearts as living tabernacles of our eucharistic Jesus, and then visit Him often with acts of adoration, love, and gratitude; this is what divine love will teach us.

When a prince sends one of his ministers to a distant country, he provides him with all that is necessary for safely reaching his destination: the Lord, my God and my Father, has given me, as my viaticum, His only Son.

III. Prayer.

Prayer is the sure way that leads to holiness.

Alas! we easily enter on the road to perdition when we neglect prayer. The prayer which humbles the soul, which inflames her with love and excites her to the practice of virtue, is never subject to illusion.

In prayer the soul is united to God through love.

He who, on account of the duties of his state of life, cannot devote much time to prayer, need not be troubled; the exact fulfillment of his duties, with a pure intention, having only God in view, is an excellent prayer.

IV. The Presence of God.

By habitually thinking of the presence of God, we succeed in prayer twenty-four hours a day.

The continual remembrance of the presence of God engenders in the soul a divine state.

V. Sin.

How can we sin with the cross of Jesus before our eyes!

VI. Faith.

Walk in faith.

The true way of holiness is the way of faith. He who walks in pure faith abandons himself into the hands of God, as a child in its mother's arms.

VII. Hope.

Hope is obligatory. I must, then, hope for my salvation. When our sins frighten us, and we fear lest we should be damned, let us think of the merits of Jesus crucified, and hope will reanimate our spirit. Let us firmly trust that, through the infinite merits of Christ's Passion and the dolors of Mary, we shall forever sing the mercies of the Most High.

VIII. Charity towards God.

The love of God is a jealous love. One atom of irregular affection for creatures suffices to ruin everything. He who would become a great saint must labor that God alone may live in him. He will have attained this end when he performs all his actions for the love of God, in union with those of

Christ, Who is our way, our truth, and our life. The heart of the true servant of God ought to be an altar whereon is daily offered the gold of charity, the incense of continual and humble prayer, and the myrrh of incessant mortification.

*

In hell, never to see God, ever to be deprived of God! Oh, what a dreadful necessity to hate Him eternally Who has loved us from all eternity!

Ever keep the fire of charity burning on the altar of your heart.

IX. Charity towards our Neighbor.

He who considers, in the light of faith and in the Heart of our divine Redeemer, the priceless value of souls, spares neither labor, nor suffering, nor perils, to aid and succor them in their spiritual needs.

Let your heart be full of compassion for the poor, and lovingly assist them, because the name of Jesus is engraven on their countenance.

When you have not the means of helping your neighbor, recommend him fervently to God, Whose sovereign dominion holds all creatures in His hand.

Counsels gently given heal every wound, but given with asperity only serve to aggravate it tenfold.

*

Be gentle in your actions; speak with a peaceful mind and in a calm tone, and you will succeed better.

Poverty is good, but charity is better.

X. Poverty.

Poverty, so much abhorred by the world, is a precious pearl, and in the sight of God contains all wealth.

Oh, what happiness we find in a community life! A precious treasure is enclosed in a community life.

My crucified Jesus, I protest that I desire not the things of the earth; for Thou alone sufficest for me, Thou alone, my God and my All!

XI. Chastity.

In order to preserve holy purity it is necessary to love it much, to distrust one's self, to be cautious with all—in a word, it is necessary to fear and to fly.

To him who loves holy purity conversations with persons

of the opposite sex always appear long and fatiguing, however short they be.

Prayer, pious reading, the frequentation of the sacraments, and, especially, the shunning of idleness, are the guardians of holy purity.

He who does not mortify his palate will neither know how to mortify his flesh.

How pure and stainless should be the heart on which is written the most holy name of Jesus!

XII. Obedience.

When there is question of obeying, we must bow our head. Let us put ourselves so entirely into the hands of our superiors that they can do with us what they will, provided they enjoin nothing opposed to the divine law. Unless we act thus, we can never taste the sweetness of God's service.

Long, as the stag panting for the waters, to have your will broken, and regard that day as lost on which you have not subjected your will to that of another.

The more obedient you are, the more tranquil and indifferent will you be as to employments that may be assigned to you.

He who is truly obedient will be better disposed and more capable to aid, by his prayers, holy Church and the religious order to which he may belong; for Jesus hears the prayer of those who are obedient.

XIII. Humility.

The least grain of pride is sufficient to overturn a mountain of holiness; allow yourself, there-fore, to be penetrated by a deep

sense of your own misery. Be dead
to all that is not God; keep yourself
detached from every creature, in
perfect interior solitude. All this
will be easy to you if you make
yourself little, for God loves childlike souls, and teaches them that
exalted wisdom which is hidden
from the wise of this world.

XIV. The Will of God.

Let us desire nothing so
much as the good pleasure of God.

As soon as we know the will
of God, we ought without delay to
follow it.

When our pious under-
takings meet with little success, let
us not be troubled; when God
wills anything to be done for His
glory He will not fail to urge on
the work until it is accomplished.

XV. Confidence in God.

If our salvation depended only on ourselves, we should have much to fear; but as it is in the hands of God, we can tranquilly repose in Him.

He that rises after his falls, with confidence in God and profound humility of heart, will become, in God's hands, a proper instrument for the accomplishment of great things; but he who acts otherwise can never do any good.

Let us never despair of the divine help; we would thereby do a serious injustice to the Father of mercies.

We must watch over ourselves. We must have the most filial confidence in Our Saviour, in our blessed Mother, in the angels and saints; but as for men, we must avoid them: this is the advice of the angel to St. Arsenius. Have courage; be assured that God will never abandon you, but will always assist you and give you what is needful.

Look at St. Theresa: obstacles served only to inflame her ardor in the establishment of her monasteries; opposition was to her a presage of the glory that works thus combated give to God.

XVI. Love of Sufferings

The soul is a seed which God sows in the field of the Church; to produce fruits, it must die under the strokes of pains, sorrows, contradictions, and persecutions.

*

The greater our cross, the greater is our gain; the more deprived suffering is of consolation, the purer is it; the more creatures are against us, the more closely united are we to God.

*

He who truly loves God regards as little what he suffers for God's sake.

*

In your trials, have recourse to Mary, and she will remedy them.

*

Do you know why God subjects you to so many miseries? That He may bestow on you the riches of heaven.

*

Suffering is brief; joy will be eternal.

*

Let us fear more to be deprived of sufferings than a miser fears to lose his treasures.

*

Sufferings are the pearls of Jesus crucified.

*

It happens sometimes that the lightning rends a mountain and discloses therein a mine of gold. So, also, the thunderbolts of adversity discover a gold-mine in certain souls.

XVII. Detachment from Self.

Happy the soul that is detached from self-satisfaction, from her own will, from her own sentiments!

*

Self-love is a dragon of seven heads; it seeks to insert them, everywhere; hence we must always fear it, and guard ourselves against it.

Esteem what belongs to another, and despise what belongs to yourself.

*

We must persuade ourselves that we are nothing, that we can do nothing, that we know nothing.

*

To have nothing, to be able to do nothing, to know nothing! and God will cause to spring from this nothingness the work of His greatest glory.

XVIII. Death.

Whenever death inspires me with fear, I dissipate it immediately in the Passion of my Redeemer.

*

In reality, to die is sweet, rather than. bitter. Death is but the privation of life, which is taken from us by the same God Who gave it.

*

I accept death willingly. He who is guilty of high treason should die; I am guilty, therefore it is just that I die. After a momentary suffering, divine mercy reserves for you endless joy.

*

Tell me: what would you fain have done were you to die now? Would you have lived in luxury, which usually leads to grievous sins, and be cast into hell, or would you rather have led a poor life, and wing your flight to heaven?

APPENDIX.

Method of Meditating.

Preparation.

Retire, if possible, to some place where you can pray in silence and recollection.

Kneel down and recollect yourself in the presence of God; adore His infinite majesty; humble yourself before Him; beg pardon for your sins; implore His grace, saying some prayer like the following: "Grant me, O Lord, through Thy bitter Passion and death, the grace to know and love Thy infinite goodness; to thank Thee and compassionate Thee for Thy sufferings in my behalf. Awaken in me a lively sorrow for my sins and help me for the future to do Thy holy will."

You may also invoke the assistance of Mary, of your patron saint, and other saints to whom you have a special devotion.

Body of the Meditation.

Now read or recall to mind some part of the Passion on which you wish to meditate, such as the agony of Our Lord in the garden, the crowning with thorns, the scourging, or the crucifixion.

Consider, then, Our Lord's sufferings, comprising them under the following simple questions:

1. Who is it that suffers?
2. What does He suffer?
3. Why does He suffer?
4. How does He suffer?

Dwell for some time on each one of these points. Consider: First, as to who it is that suffers; that He is God—Lord of all, Creator of all, God incarnate, Redeemer, infinitely perfect, good, kind, just, loving, etc. Make some acts of adoration, love, veneration, etc.

Secondly, as to what He suffers: consider the cruelty, shamefulness, length, excess of suffering, etc., and make repeated acts of regret, sorrow, compassion, etc.

Thirdly, as to why He suffers; reflect that it is not for His own sake, but for men, His creatures, for sinners especially, and therefore for you in particular.

Consider, then, your little-ness, unworthiness, guilt, ingrati-tude, etc., and humble yourself before God, and thank Him for His infinite love, etc.

Moreover, consider that He also suffered to give you an example of virtue, to teach you the malice of sin, to withdraw you from vice, etc. and then recall to mind the special vices or faults to which you are subject; beg pardon of God and resolve to amend; adopt some special means, etc.

Fourthly, consider how, or in what manner, Jesus suffers. Reflect on the special virtues of which He gives you an example: His meekness, silence, obedience, patience, etc.; and see how you can imitate Him, or receive encouragement from Him.

Conclusion.

Conclude your pious reflections by resolving to practice some particular virtue, or to avoid some habitual fault, for the sake of your suffering Lord, in imitation of His example; and thank Him for the grace and light He has bestowed upon you. Pray earnestly for His constant assistance in trials and temptations; beg Our Lord for any spiritual or temporal benefit you stand in need of; remember also to pray for all that have a special claim on you, and finish by devoutly and slowly reciting an *Our Father, Hail Mary,* and *Glory be to the Father.* Take some little maxim or devout thought with you from your meditation, and endeavor to recall it frequently to mind during the day.

Outlines of Some Meditations on the Passion.

I. Prayer and Agony of Jesus in the Garden.

"And being in agony, He prayed the longer. And His sweat became as drops of blood trickling down upon the ground." (Luke xxii. 43, 44).

Consider:

1. The natural fear and anguish of Jesus at the near approach of His Passion—how each of His impending torments rises distinctly before Him. Compassionate Him in His agony.

2. His hatred of sin, the clearness with which He sees its malice and deformity, the enormous multitude and wickedness of all the sins of the world laid upon

Him. Reflect that He is the Son of God, innocence and sanctity itself, and that He has an infinite hatred of sin; hence gather what pain it caused Him to take them upon Himself.

3. His infinite love and goodness towards men, shown by willingly accepting the burden of their sins; His submission to His Father's will, His resignation, earnestness and perseverance in prayer.

Conceive a tender compassion for Him, a hatred and detestation of sin, and grieve for your own sins, so heinous in the sight of God. Resolve never to commit sin any more, to pray earnestly and perseveringly to God for assistance; watch and pray, and prepare for temptation.

II. Jesus Betrayed to His Enemies by Judas.

"Behold a multitude: and he that was called Judas, one of the twelve, went before them, and drew near to Jesus, for to kiss Him. And Jesus said to him: Judas, dost thou betray the Son of man with a kiss?" (Luke xxii. 47, 48).

Consider:

1. The pain inflicted on Jesus by the malice and ingratitude of Judas; His grief at the treason of so favored a disciple.

2. The gentleness of Jesus, and His readiness to forgive He calls His traitor "Friend." What mercy and compassion! So He addresses you when you would commit sin; He endeavors to recall you by goodness, mercy, etc. How often have you sinned, notwithstanding!

3. The obduracy of Judas: he is not even moved by the loving kindness of Jesus.

Let Judas be a warning to you; fear familiarity with sin, which hardens the heart and leads to final impenitence. Condole with Jesus in His grief; learn of Him gentleness, kindness, readiness to forgive, etc.

III. Jesus Insulted and Condemned by the Chief Priests.

"What think you? But they answering said: He is guilty of death. Then did they spit in His face, and buffeted Him, and others struck His face with the palms of their hands." (Matt. xxvi. 66, 67).

Consider:

1. The confusion and pain of Jesus to be thus treated by the ancients and the priests; the insults

and blows He receives; how unjustly condemned to death.

2. The hypocrisy of the Jews; their arrogance, pride, etc.; their impieties, blasphemies, falsehoods, etc.

3. The silence, forbearance, and patience of Jesus. What an example of meekness! He endures this ignominy in silence to atone for our murmurs when justly reproved, etc.

Adore the infinite goodness of God bearing patiently such contempt for your sake. Make reparation for the insults He receives; grieve for your own sins, which are infinitely offensive to God. Pray to be delivered from all pride, arrogance, hypocrisy, etc.; conceive a hatred of blasphemy and pray to prevent it.

IV. Jesus before Pilate.

"And they brought Him bound, and delivered Him to Pontius Pilate the governor...And he had then a notorious prisoner, called Barabbas. They therefore being gathered together, Pilate said: Whom will you that I release to you: Barabbas, or Jesus that is called Christ?...But they said: Barabbas." (Matt. xxvii. 2, 16, 17, 21).

Consider:

1. The sufferings of Jesus when dragged from tribunal to tribunal; the contempt with which Pilate regarded Him; the ignominy of Jesus, the innocent Lamb, in being compared to a robber and murderer.

2. The injustice of Pilate; the iniquity of the Jews clamoring for Barabbas. How often have you

done the same, yielding to vile passions, choosing sin instead of God!

3. The love of Jesus for our poor souls enslaved by sin. He willingly remains bound to deliver us from the bondage of sin. We sinners are released, while Jesus dies for us.

Resolve to imitate the love of Jesus; to be kind, self-sacrificing, loving towards others. Conceive a sincere shame and confusion for wishing to be esteemed more than others. Often reflect on the charity of Jesus delivering Himself to death for you.

V. Jesus Derided by Herod.

"And Herod with his army set Him at naught, and mocked Him, putting on Him a white garment." (Luke xxiii. 11).

Consider:

1. The outrage committed by Herod on the wisdom, innocence, and holiness of Jesus.

2. The iniquity of the Jews assisting at this mockery of their Saviour.

3. The composure, meek and silent endurance of Jesus. He atones for our pride, vanity, etc.

Learn, hence, the value of innocence; regret your foolish esteem of the things of the world; henceforth esteem everything else vain but the virtue and innocence of Jesus. Grieve for the insults Jesus here suffered; adore His wisdom, truth, and sanctity.

VI. Jesus Scourged.

"Then Pilate took Jesus, and scourged Him." (John xix. 1).

Consider:

1. The virginal body of Jesus torn and mangled by the scourges; the intense pain He endures; His exhaustion, loss of blood, etc.; His confusion at such exposure, etc.

2. The manner in which He bears this humiliation. What patience, meekness, etc. His charity and mercy towards us; He bears the wounds we deserve for our sins.

3. The cause of this special suffering; our many secret sins; our luxury, softness, pride, and pampering of the body; our shameful nakedness before God, etc.

Compassionate Jesus bearing so many stripes weep for your own offenses, your love of ease, luxury, etc. Resolve henceforth to check the indulgence of the flesh by mortification, self-denial, constancy in prayer, etc.

VII. Jesus Crowned with Thorns.

"And the soldiers platting a crown of thorns, put it upon His head: and they put on Him a purple garment." (John xix. 2).

Consider:

1. The sacred head of Jesus suffering the most excruciating torture. What an agony for Jesus! Think how painful would even one thorn be to you.

2. The mockery and insolence of the soldiers putting on Him a purple garment; their cruelty; the malignant taunts, etc., of the Jews.

3. The submission, meekness, and patience of Jesus; how severely He atones for our sins of thought, for our wanton complacency in evil, etc.

Grieve for the sufferings inflicted on Jesus; adore Him as

your Lord; admire His patience,
love, etc. Nevermore indulge in
sinful thoughts, in pride, arrogance, and evil desires; imitate the
humility, submission, etc., of Jesus.

VIII. Jesus carrying His Cross.

"And bearing His own cross
He went forth to that place which
is called Calvary, but in Hebrew
Golgotha." (John xix. 17).

Consider:

1. The long and painful way;
the prolonged sufferings and
fatigue of Jesus; the Pharisees,
priests, and the multitude driving
Him on with taunts, blows,
execrations, etc. Such was the
reward He received from men for
His works of love and mercy.

2. The manner in which Jesus
accepts His cross—His alacrity,
joy, submission, etc. He shows

how we are to follow Him in carrying our cross gladly and patiently.

3. The comfort He derived amid so many sufferings from the fidelity of Mary, His Mother; the compassion of the holy women and others who wept for Him.

Resolve to repent sincerely, and grieve for your sins; they laid this heavy cross on Jesus. Take courage from His example to bear your own cross willingly. Your only way to heaven is by the way of the cross. Deny yourself, take up your cross, and follow Him.

IX. The Crucifixion of Jesus.

"And they gave Him to drink wine mingled with myrrh: but He took it not. And crucifying Him, they divided His garments." (Mark xv. 23, 24).

Consider:

1.   The   contempt   and
ignominy surrounding Jesus; the
cruelty of the soldiers offering Him
such a bitter drink; His previous
wounds, sufferings, fatigue, etc.

2. The tender hands and feet
of Jesus pierced by iron nails.
What pain and agony He endures
on the hard bed of the cross!
Compassionate your Lord. How
easy is it to sin. But see what it cost
Jesus to atone for your sins; look at
His bleeding, mangled hands and
feet.

3. The obedience of Jesus
unto the death of the cross; His
patience   and   silence   when
stretching out His hands to be
nailed to the cross, a victim for
your sins.

Deplore your sins that drove
those cruel nails into the hands
and feet of Jesus. Learn from Jesus,
stretched bleeding on the cross,

what an evil sin is in the sight of God, since it requires such an atonement. Thank Him for all He has suffered for you; learn to make some sacrifice for His sake; abandon some predominant vice, etc.; never say that too much is required of you; in all trials imitate the sublime virtues of Jesus, His obedience, patience, etc.

X. Agony and Death of Jesus on the Cross.

"And the sun was darkened: and the veil of the temple was rent in the midst. And Jesus, crying with a loud voice, said: Father, into Thy hands I commend my spirit. And saying this, He gave up the ghost." (Luke xxiii. 45, 46).

Consider:

1. The prolonged agony of Jesus on the cross, sustained

meekly and patiently for three hours; the constant increase of pain in His wounds; His desolation when forsaken by His Father; His thirst quenched with vinegar.

2. The insults and mockery heaped upon Him to the last moment; the merciless taunts, curses, and blasphemies of the soldiers. What anguish their sins cause Him!

3. His charity and kindness even to His enemies; His last and greatest example of love and mercy; His tender and consoling words to His sorrowing Mother, John, and the good thief; His last cry to His Father. Thus Jesus dies for you.

Kneel in spirit at the foot of the cross; there weep for your sins; weep for the long and painful sufferings they inflicted on Jesus. Weep with Mary, John, and

Magdalen for His death. Here at last learn to love and nevermore to offend so good a Master.

XI. The Burial of Jesus.

"Now there was in the place, where He was crucified, a garden: and in the garden a new sepulchre, wherein no man yet had been laid. There, therefore, they laid Jesus." (John xix. 41).

Consider:

1. The sacred lifeless body of Jesus laid in a tomb. What a mystery of love and mercy, that the Son of God should be thus buried in a strange, lowly tomb, mourned by His own creatures!

2. The bereavement and desolation of Mary and the friends of Jesus; with Him, the life and light of the world, their hope seemed dead.

3. The door of the sepulchre is closed. Jesus is also no longer with us; He shall no longer live and speak with us. What an evil has sin done! It drove us from paradise; now it has also deprived us of Jesus.

Mourn at the sepulchre of Jesus for your own sins; here bury yourself with Jesus; bury your sins, at least, in true contrition, that you may rise to a new life.

XII. The Sorrows of Mary.

"Now there stood by the cross of Jesus His Mother." (John xix. 25).

Consider:
1. The tender, loving Mother of Jesus, overwhelmed with grief at the foot of the cross; the anguish of her maternal heart at the sight of the nails, the thorns, the wounds

and mortal agony of Jesus, her Son her helplessness at the foot of the cross.

2. Her innocence, love and devotion to Jesus; how the tumult and cries of His enemies around the cross afflict her; how cruelly they who crucify her Son by sin wound her, etc.

3. Her constancy and fidelity; her compassion for her Son; her desire to suffer with Him, to relieve Him, and her grief for sin. How sublime are her resignation and her imitation of the virtues of Jesus—of His submission, patience, charity, etc.!

Resolve never to forget the sorrows of your heavenly Mother. Condole and sympathize with her sorrowing heart; place yourself by her side at the foot of the cross, and learn of her to imitate, love, and serve Jesus; to hate and grieve for sin; to fear the justice of God; to set a true value on your soul. Implore her intercession in all your necessities.

Short Method of Reciting the Beads of the Five Wounds of Jesus

V. Incline unto my aid, O God.

R. O Lord, make haste to help me.

V. Glory be to the Father, and to the Son, and to the Holy Ghost.

R. As it was in the beginning, is now, and ever shall be, world without end. Amen.

> Holy Mother! pierce me through;
> In my heart each wound renew
> Of my Saviour crucified.

First Wound—The Left Foot.

My crucified Jesus, I devoutly adore the painful wound of Thy left foot. Ah! by the pain which Thou didst endure therein, and by the blood which Thou didst shed from that foot, grant me grace to fly the occasions of sin, and not to walk in the way of iniquity, which leads to perdition.

Glory be to the Father, and to the Son, and to the Holy Ghost, etc., five times.

One *Hail Mary* and *Holy Mother! pierce me*, etc., as above.

Second Wound—The Right Foot.

My crucified Jesus, I devoutly adore the painful wound of Thy right foot. Ah! by the pain which Thou didst endure therein, and by the blood which Thou didst shed from that foot, grant me grace to walk constantly in the way of Christian virtue, even to the entrance of paradise.

Glory be to the Father, etc., five times.

One *Hail Mary* and *Holy Mother! pierce me*, etc., as above.

Third Wound—The Left Hand.

My crucified Jesus, I devoutly adore the painful wound of Thy left hand. Ah! by the pain which Thou didst endure therein, and by the blood which Thou didst shed from that hand, deliver me from being found at Thy left hand, with the reprobate, at the Last Judgment.

Glory be to the Father, etc., five times.

One *Hail Mary* and *Holy Mother! pierce me*, etc., as above.

Fourth Wound—The Right Hand.

My crucified Jesus, I devoutly adore the painful wound of Thy right hand. Ah! by the pain which Thou didst endure therein, and by the blood which Thou didst shed from that hand, bless my soul, and conduct it to Thy kingdom.

Glory be to the Father, etc., five times.

One *Hail Mary* and *Holy Mother! pierce me,* etc., as above.

Fifth Wound—The Side.

My crucified Jesus, I devoutly adore the wound in Thy sacred side. Ah! by the blood which Thou didst shed from it, enkindle in my heart the fire of Thy love, and give me grace to persevere in loving Thee for all eternity.

Glory be to the Father, etc., five times.

One *Hail Mary* and *Holy Mother! pierce me,* etc., as above.

Short Prayer to the Virgin of Sorrows.

O afflicted Mother! O virginal heart, all buried in the wounds of thy Son! accept this short memorial of His pains in union with thy grief. Present to Jesus this act of homage, and render my prayers available by thy intercession. Amen.

Three *Hail Marys,* etc.

Chaplet or Beads of the Seven Dolors.

This is a devotion instituted in the course of the thirteenth century, in honor of the sorrows of the Blessed Virgin Mary, endured by her in compassion for the suffering and death of her Divine Son. It is practiced upon a chaplet composed of seven times seven beads, each portion of seven being divided from the rest by medals representing the seven principal sorrows of her life. In the use of it a *Hail Mary* has to be said on each of the beads with one *Our Father* before every seven *Hail Marys*; and at the end of all, three *Hail Marys* are to be said, in honor of the sorrowful tears of Our Lady.

At the first medal reflect on and sympathize in the sorrow of our blessed Lady when she presented her Divine Child in the

Temple, and heard from the aged Simeon that a sword of grief should pierce her soul on His account.

Our Father, seven *Hail Marys.*

At the second medal, reflect on her sorrow when, to escape the cruelty of King Herod, she was forced to fly into Egypt with St. Joseph and her beloved Child.

Our Father, seven *Hail Marys.*

At the third medal, reflect on her grief when, in returning from Jerusalem, she perceived that she had lost her dear Jesus, Whom she sought sorrowing during three days.

Our Father, seven *Hail Marys.*

At the fourth medal, reflect on her anguish when, on the road, she beheld her Divine Son borne down by the weight of the cross.

Our Father, seven *Hail Marys.*

At the fifth medal, reflect on her unutterable woe in seeing her beloved Son die, in untold agony, on the cross.

  Our Father, seven *Hail Marys*.

  At the sixth medal, reflect on the sword of sorrow that pierced her tender heart when the cruel soldier thrust his lance into the sacred side of her Jesus.

  Our Father, seven *Hail Marys*.

  At the seventh medal, reflect on the sense of loneliness and desolation that filled this most loving Mother's heart when Jesus was laid in the sepulchre.

  Our Father, seven *Hail Marys*.

The Way of the Cross before a Crucifix.

The Way of the Cross makes easy meditating on the sufferings of Our Saviour. The Holy See, wishing to encourage this excellent method, has granted many indulgences to those who piously perform it. Since there may be some who cannot visit a church in which the Stations of the Cross are erected, such as the sick or those who are on the sea, in prisons, or living among infidels, the Holy See has granted the same indulgences to these, provided that they recite, with at least contrite heart and devotion, before a crucifix blessed by a priest who has this special faculty, twenty times the *Our Father, Hail Mary,* and *Glory be to the Father*—namely, one *Our Father,* etc., for each Station of the

Cross, five in memory of the wounds of Our Lord Jesus Christ, and one according to the intention of the Sovereign Pontiff.—*Decree,* 16th September, 1859.

Moreover, those who, on account of sickness, are unable to recite the twenty *Our Fathers,* etc., can gain the same indulgences by reciting an act of contrition, or the invocation: "We therefore beseech Thee to assist Thy servants, whom Thou hast redeemed by Thy precious blood."—*Pontifical Brief,* 18th December, 1877.

It is to be observed that the crucifixes must be of material not easily broken; as also that they thus indulgenced cannot be sold, or given away, or lent to any one for the purpose of gaining the indulgences.

Ejaculations.

My Jesus, mercy.—100 days indulgence each time.

My sweetest Jesus, be not my Judge, but my Saviour.—50 days indulgence each time.

Jesus, my God, I love Thee above all things.—50 days each time.

Prayer before a Crucifix after Communion.

Look down upon me, O good and gentle Jesus, while before Thy face I humbly kneel and with burning soul pray and beseech Thee to fix deeply in my heart lively sentiments of faith, hope, and charity, true contrition for my sins, and a firm purpose of amendment; while I contemplate with great love and tender pity

Thy five wounds, pondering over them within me, and call to mind the words which David the prophet said of Thee, my Jesus: "They pierced My hands and My feet, they numbered all My bones." (Ps. xxi. 11, 18).

Plenary indulgence if said with a penitent heart after confession and Communion. Some time must also be spent in praying for the intention of His Holiness.

Acknowledgements

With gratitude to the benefactors of
Filii Passionis permitting the publication of
these works to spread devotion to the Passion of Our Lord Jesus Christ.

Other works by Filii Passionis:

Saint Gabriel of Our Lady of Sorrows:
Compilation

Meditations from the School of
Jesus Crucified
by Father Ignatius of the Side of Jesus, CP

Explanation of the Holy Mass
by Dom Prosper Guéranger, OSB

Praying the Mass During Advent: Excerpts
from the Liturgical Year
by Dom Prosper Guéranger, OSB

Made in the USA
Columbia, SC
03 March 2025